D0309122

THE
WEINSTEINS'
WAR

THE
WEINSTEINS' WAR

*Letters of Love,
Struggle and Survival*

RUTH MENDICK
& JEREMY WEINSTEIN

Northamptonshire
Libraries & Information
Service
KR

Askews & Holts	2 0 1 2

First published 2012
by Spellmount, an imprint of The History Press
The Mill, Brimscombe Port
Stroud, Gloucestershire, GL5 2QG
www.thehistorypress.co.uk

© Ruth Mendick & Jeremy Weinstein, 2012

The right of Ruth Mendick & Jeremy Weinstein
to be identified as the Authors of this work has
been asserted in accordance with the
Copyrights, Designs and Patents Act 1988.

All rights reserved. No part of this book may be reprinted
or reproduced or utilised in any form or by any electronic,
mechanical or other means, now known or hereafter invented,
including photocopying and recording, or in any information
storage or retrieval system, without the permission in writing
from the Publishers.

British Library Cataloguing in Publication Data.
A catalogue record for this book is available from the British Library.

ISBN 978 0 7524 7934 7

Typesetting and origination by The History Press
Manufacturing managed by Jellyfish Print Solutions Ltd
Printed in India.

CONTENTS

INTRODUCTION

THIS IS THE STORY of the Second World War as experienced by one young family, David and Sylvia Weinstein and their little daughter, Ruth, and discovered through the 700 or so letters that they sent to each other. The letters begin in 1942, when David first went abroad on active service (having joined up in 1940), through to his discharge home in 1946.

David's war was a busy one. As a soldier in the Eighth Army, a gunner, he fought at El Alamein in North Africa and was then at the landings in Sicily, which then led to his trek through Europe, including being part of the barrage supporting Operation Market Garden. He ended the war as a member of the Army of Occupation in Germany. As the regimental tailor, he turned up sleeves, sewed on insignia and oversaw the work of a group of Germans who were part of his team. Here he had a coat made for Ruth: it was too big for her but she would 'grow into it', he writes, a metaphor, perhaps, for his life in the services. He survived, even thrived, by developing physically, socially and psychologically, growing into his uniform so that it fit every contour of his being, with a tucking-in here and an addition there. David was at times enormously proud of what he had become, and sometimes he felt distinctly uncomfortable. His letters provide fascinating insights into the battles he fights and also the extraordinary ordinariness of the routine life of a soldier. He continually observed and commented upon the cities, towns and villages he passed through and the people he met: refugees, families he was billeted upon, women who turned to prostitution and black marketeers, as well as his fellow soldiers. There were some light moments alongside the grim or exciting: he helped milk cows and deliver babies, he had Sylvia send him subscriptions to socialist papers like *The Daily Worker* and *Reynold's News* and asked also for mysteries and westerns with names like *The Mystery of the Semi-Nude* and *She Strangled Her Lover* (letter dated 12.07.44).

He was helped throughout by his knowledge of Yiddish, learnt back home with his family and in the Jewish East End of London, which lent itself so well to the mix of German and Dutch that became the language of wartime Europe. This background also gave him a sharp interest in the Jewish/Palestinian soldiers that he met at various points and there is poignancy in his friendship with the German Jews he encountered on their return from the camps. These experiences, along with the marking of the various religious festivals while out in the field, even under fire, left David intensely aware of what it meant to be Jewish at this momentous time in the world's history. David kept a political eye open on all that he saw and read, and showed his intense excitement for the post-war Britain, and Europe, that was emerging. Having helped achieve the victory in war, the letters end with him anticipating the part that he and Sylvia can play in helping a Labour Britain win the peace.

Sylvia's war, on the Home Front, was no less eventful or dangerous. In retrospect we know that the worst of the Blitz was over, but her letters reveal the continuing fear of danger, death and destruction from the skies and the constant struggle to adjust to and cope with the deprivations and fears of what has been termed the first example of 'total war'. An especially significant factor for Sylvia was that she had recently left, or escaped, her large, close but complicated family after becoming a wife and a mother and sharing a business with David. Then, in April 1941, they were bombed out and she found herself back with her family. This was initially with her sister Fay, in Ilford, in a small premises above a grocer's shop that had to be shared with Fay's own young family, two boys aged 5 and 7 plus a sister-in-law, Betty, aged 19. David and Sam, Fay's husband, were also there when on leave from the army. Sylvia and Ruth then moved, in 1944, to Frome, Somerset, where other family members had gone to escape the London bombings. Sylvia finally returned to set up home in Walthamstow, still in East London. While much of the literature about women in the war is about how they found new, transformational roles for themselves, either in such settings as the Land Army or in work (as in the iconic figure of 'Rosie the Riveter' (also see the accounts collected by Nicholson, 2011)), Sylvia's was a more internal, domestic struggle to survive; she describes herself as 'the odd one' in her family (08.12.42), managing what we would now call a single-parent family. She organised rations, dealt with the continued bombings, negotiated with the authorities and weathered the tensions and rivalries within her wider family, while parenting her own daughter and sustaining Ruth's muddled relationship with a father that was missing at such a crucial time in her young life as she grew from being a toddler to having her first day at school.

Both David and Sylvia had an urgent need to share the details of their own world and to know as much as possible of their spouse's experiences – to enter their parallel life as fully as possible. Thus David seized on the smallest details of Sylvia's domestic circumstances and of Ruth's development while Sylvia listened to the radio, followed the papers, watched the newsreels and equally avidly awaited and devoured David's letters. They used the letters as best they could to continue the intimate relationship of a still-new marriage that had been so rudely interrupted by the war and which no one knew when or if it would be resumed. This is a conversation about war, religion and politics as well as the more intimate aspects of family, love and sexual longing. The importance of the correspondence is most eloquently expressed by David and Sylvia themselves. Thus Sylvia writes how 'it does seem to bring us closer to one another. I can feel your presence ... when I read those dear letters that you write these days' (03.05.43), while David refers to how 'I can have spiritual contact with you by writing' (19.05.43). In the extracts that follow David's spelling has not been corrected – he jokingly defends his spelling as 'modern' against Sylvia's 'old fashioned' approach (21.08.45).

While the letters provide a very striking story of their lives and struggles they do not, of course, provide a complete story. At their most basic they can be just a tick-box affair. A pre-prepared letter (27.10.44) from the senior Jewish chaplain leaves spaces for the Revd Levy to write in 'Mrs Weinstein', followed by the typed 'I have to-day seen', with 'your husband' again there by hand, followed by the typed 'I am sure you will be pleased to know that I found him well and in good spirits'. The reverend does apologise for the 'very impersonal form of note'. David sends (07.07.45) a field service postcard, which has a number of phrases that can be struck out as appropriate. The choice includes such bald statements as 'been admitted to hospital because of sickness or wounds', 'a letter, telegram and/or parcel has been received' or complaining that 'no letter has been received' either 'lately' or 'not at all'. David ticks the message 'I am quite well, letter follows at first opportunity'. There were telegrams for urgent news, airgraphs which were very short and so necessarily to the point, letter-cards and, most valued in terms of length, airmail letters, which could take four to five months to reach their destination. Sylvia and David were clear about their preferences, David writing (20.12.42) that:

> [Y]our air-graphs are very sweet tasters, but your letters are like a jolly good feed, and though they take so long & contain old news, never-the-less they are more than welcome.

The letters were also written in the shadow of the censor. The unit commander was expected to scrutinise all correspondence to prevent the leaking of sensitive military information and to assess the mood of the men. Consequently soldiers tended to entrust their more personal thoughts to 'the green envelopes' which were less often opened at source, and, even then, would be opened by the base commander who was more distant from the men and so was less likely to know them personally. There was also self-censorship, giving the letters a cautionary feel as they struggled to find a way to talk to each other about their fears, frustrations and intimacies. David apologises (23.09.44), wishing that he 'had the nack of expressing my-self', while Sylvia (18.08.42) comments:

> Anyway, Davie, it is rather awkward being intimate with a piece of paper, if you get my meaning. – But I do usually write what I want to, & who cares who reads it.

The self-censorship is also seen in how much time David needed to tell the full story; thus he describes a battle he was in, what we now know as Operation Market Garden, but it was a while before the censor allowed him to give a fuller set of details and it then took further time before David felt able to disclose the personal impact that the battle had on him. David was careful sometimes in what he wrote and hurt his wife when she found the phrase 'don't tell Sylvia' in a letter to another family member (08.12.42). David and Sylvia also experienced frustrations when letters were delayed because of bad weather or rapid troop movements, or when others got damaged in transit or were lost completely.

For all their limitations, however, the letters represent a fascinating account and both David and Sylvia seem to have been aware of the significance of what they were writing. David comments (23.09.44) that his could be 'the basis of one of the greatest books yet to be written' and (02.02.43) that Sylvia's letters read:

> almost like a book. When I get back home P.G. [abbreviation for 'Please God'] I shall have them printed as a book and title it 'The Memoirs of a soldiers wife'. It will amuse Ruth in later years they are certainly an enfolding tale of a child's early development, as well as the fears, hopes & future of an anxious loving wife.

What follows, then, serves as the book that neither wrote but could and perhaps should have done. We, the editors, the children of David and Sylvia, have drawn on the letters, taking up what seem to be the most important themes for a wider readership, using always the words of David and Sylvia themselves but with footnotes at the end of each chapter if readers are interested in a wider context. There are also the memories of those all too few family members who shared this momentous point in history.

One

PERSONAL HISTORIES

PERSONAL HISTORIES SKETCHES OUT David and Sylvia's family backgrounds and their lives up to the outbreak of war. It also suggests the influences of the Jewish East End on their subsequent experiences of war.

David was the son of Hyman Vashan, born in Balta, a village near Odessa, in 1884, and of Sima Elezatsky, six years younger than her husband and from a village 100 miles north-east of Moscow. They came to London at the turn of the century, part of a wave of Jewish immigrants fleeing pogroms and poverty, and it was at the port coming into England that an official changed their name to 'Weinstein'. Presumably, rather than struggling with the accent and lack of English, it was easier to assume that another 'Yid' from Eastern Europe must be called some variation on the name 'Stein'. Once settled, Hyman started a second-hand clothes shop. David was born in the East End of London in 1912, first living in Cable Street, later Whitechapel Street. He went to a school that still stands, and which he called 'Checker Alley' (actually Checker Street) where, he would further joke, the board celebrating pupils' achievements had fallen into dilapidation through under use. It can be assumed that David had a traditional Jewish upbringing and certainly there are a number of Biblical and religious references in his letters. When Vera, Sima's sister, died, among her possessions were some leaflets produced by the Bund, the mass Jewish socialist party in Russia and Poland, which indicates political talk in the home.

There were five children: David had one younger brother, Alf, who is often mentioned in the letters, and three sisters, Doris, Betty and Eva. Alf was single and although two of the sisters were married, they were childless; David, of course, had a child, Ruth, born in 1940 following his marriage to Sylvia in 1937. David's concern for his younger brother, who was also serving in the war, often surfaces in the letters.

Sylvia was born in 1914. Her mother, Alta Melenek, originally lived 40 miles north of Warsaw, and her father, Abraham Ruda (later known as Rudoff), was born in 1876 in Zakroczym, 50 miles north-west of Warsaw. There is a very formal photograph portrait of him as a soldier in the tsar's army. As with the Vashans/Weinsteins, the family came to Britain at the turn of the twentieth century, bringing with them the two eldest children, Millie and Belle. According to the unpublished biography of his son, Lou Ryder (Ryder, 1994), Abraham had intended to join his older brother in Argentina, but financial pressures meant that he settled for, and settled in, Cable Street. Alta had eleven children in all; two died in infancy and of the surviving ones Sylvia, born in 1916, was the second youngest. Abraham was a deeply religious man, later founding a synagogue in the unlikely setting of Frome, Somerset, in the front room of the house where they stayed during the war, and then another in Ilford. His faith led him to break off completely contact with a brother, Hymie, who was a communist and atheist. Abraham also worked as a tailor dealing in second-hand clothes ('the Shmutter trade') and some property. Sylvia refers in her letters to helping to prepare the rent books.

When Sylvia was 4 the family moved to Amhurst Road in Stoke Newington, where they stayed for ten years, and then to Highbury. However this is to jump ahead of a major disaster in the life of Sylvia and the whole family. In 1923, when Sylvia was just 7, her mother, Alta, died following a routine gallstones operation. Something of the personal impact of this is reflected in Sylvia telling the toddler Ruth, who sees the *yahtzeit* (memorial) candle burning, that 'when I was a little girl I was naughty & my mummy went away & left me' (letter to David, 31.05.43).

Life then became 'chaotic' (Ryder, 1994, p. 18). The two oldest sisters were already married so it was left to the 17-year-old Esther to run the home until Abraham married a factory worker, Sarah (ever after called 'Aunt'), and Lou comments that although Sylvia 'soon adjusted … she became very hostile later' (Ryder, 1994, p. 19).

Sylvia was very bright at school, especially at maths, gaining a scholarship at 11, but her hopes of becoming a teacher were thwarted by the family's poverty and a lack of commitment to women having a career. She left school at 16 to start work at a grocer's, a disappointment that stayed with her throughout her life.

In the letters there are frequent references to her eldest sister, Millie, who took on the matriarchal role in the family, and her son, Lionel, away in Canada training with the RAF, also provokes much comment. Sylvia's younger brothers, Lou and Ralph, are also mentioned frequently.

The East End where David and Sylvia lived is familiar from a whole host of memoirs, novels and historical studies. Lou saw it as a place of 'narrow cobbled streets, permanently muddied and generously sprinkled with horse manure. Streets where the sun was ashamed to show its face' (Ryder, 1994, p.8). Joe Jacobs describes (1978) the crowded housing and the struggle to find work, which seems to have been typical, and also an atmosphere where 'the adults sat on chairs on the pavements outside the front doors talking, laughing, arguing very excitedly during the evening and late into the night' (p.21). David was a tailor so he was likely to recognise Jacobs' description of the headquarters of the Tailors' and Garment Workers' Trade Union for Gents' Tailoring:

> There were … offices either side of the passage which led to a wider wooden staircase … there were small openings covered by panels which slid up and you talk to a face on the other side. Climbing the stairs you would hear voices often very loud above the general gabble of conversation mostly in Yiddish. In addition load bangs as the dominoes hit the table tops. On entering a very large room, occupying the whole of that floor, the cigarette smoke would almost cause you to choke. Here, during the daytime, were the men who were unemployed, to be joined in the late evenings by those who had been working. Teas and snacks of all

kinds were available, at a small bar occupying one corner. The floor above
had several rooms in which there was always some sort of meeting going
on. (p.20)

This was where David's education started, in the setting of the labour
movement, through the books of the Left Book Club, and at meetings
first of the Independent Labour Party (a form from the London and
Southern Counties Divisional Council of the ILP dated 25 July 1933
certifies that Mr David Weinstein of 102 Whitechapel Street, Finsbury
E.C. is the agent for the ILP) and then the Labour Party, whereas other
friends, including Phil who features in the wartime letters, joined the
Communist Party. David spoke at street-corner meetings with the likes
of Tom Mann, so he was at the centre of political turmoil, and Lou Ryder
describes David being struck by police batons during a demonstration
in support of the unemployed (Ryder, 1994, p.64). David leaving school
coincided with the 1926 General Strike, and the clashes with Mosley's
fascists, most famously the Battle of Cable Street in 1936 (although he
never talked about this with us, his children, or perhaps we never asked).
The concerns about fascism would inevitably play heavily on his mind,
and while the Left Book Club texts covered a whole range of political
issues, both contemporary and historical, what now stands out is a slim
volume entitled *The Jewish Question* (1937) which starts by asserting that
there is 'hardly a country under the sun where the Jew is safe from insult'
(p.7) and also a fuller book, published in 1936, that documents in close
and chilling detail the growing persecution of the Jews under the Nazis.
Its title is *The Yellow Spot: The Extermination of the Jews in Germany*.

It is important to give this background because the David we see in
the letters has all the energy and passion of his East End youth, in all its
complexity of religion, politics, culture and family life. There is an urge to
meet people and get to know them.

Sylvia was also a part of this political atmosphere, inevitably so since
she was courting and then married to David while her brother Lou was
also active in socialist politics. Lou later chose to become a conscientious
objector, so we can assume that, as war approached, there were arguments
about pacifism. The letters illustrate her political take on the war and
there is anger when she witnesses Jim Crow racism directed against black

GIs. When the country prepares for the 1945 General Election she reports back to David on the Labour Party meetings she attends.

Sylvia and David came together as a mix of the two families, the Weinsteins and the Rudoffs, with David's sister, Doris, marrying Sylvia's brother (subsequently made even more confusing when, post-war, David's brother Alf married Sylvia's niece, Evelyn, the daughter of Millie). As Sylvia describes it (18.05.43) she and David had been 'at the "walking out" stage for years, & even then were engaged for fifteen months before we were married'. They eventually married in 1937, combining what David described (31.07.45) as 'the Weinstein temperament, taking things as they come' with the 'brains' that come from the 'Rudoff family'. Ruth was born in 1940 and they set up in business, which also served as a home since they lived in a flat above the shop, but they were bombed out in 1941. David was then sent abroad with the army in 1942. From this point on the letters continue the tale.

Two

1942
AT WAR IN EGYPT, EMBATTLED AT HOME

I N THESE EARLY LETTERS we see David and Sylvia getting into a rhythm of writing, finding a style that will see them through the war. They describe the emerging rituals that will keep them in tune with each other. Sylvia shares details of Ruth growing up, the nature of her shared home with her sister and her family and the restrictions of life in London, where she was always at risk, whether from predatory men, dead mice in the bath or the continuing menace of German bombs. David gives vivid details of his 12,000-mile boat journey from the UK to Tufic on the Suez Canal and then his often quite contradictory impressions of Egypt and especially Cairo. He sees action at the Battle of El Alamein and ends 1942 exhausted and recuperating in hospital in Alexandria.

• Starting Off: Finding the Rhythm and the Rituals of Absence •

At this point Sylvia and Ruth, aged 2, had been bombed out of their own home and business, and were living in Ilford in a small premises above a grocer's shop, which had to be shared with her sister, Fay, Fay's own young family, Jeffrey and Tony, aged 5 and 7, plus a young sister-in-law, Betty, aged 19. David and Fay's husband, Sam, would also be there when on leave from the army. Jeffrey recalls the premises being on two floors –

three including the shop. Apart from the bedrooms there was a kitchen with a bath in it, a front room which was 'for best', and so never used, and a dining room in which they played, lived and ate. The cupboard under the stairs served as a shelter during air raids.

David was posted in Bromley during this initial stage of his army life and home leave, and the telephone meant that the letters lost their importance as a means of keeping in touch. There is one, dated 23 February 1942, which is six pages long, pencil written and following a leave of:

> two days and one night ... Baby was grand, and I have a feeling that this time she really did miss me ... It's a grand feeling to have a woman excite me like you do ... and I feel honoured to think that I satisfy all your demands.

David writes about the pain of being apart and tells Sylvia 'to keep your chin up ... PG when all this is over, this world will be for us and us alone'. What follows are some travel details and then he is returns to his love for the family: 'I'm a happy man, it's great to have such a wife and baby.'

Similar themes are in his letter dated 25 May 1942, but of a different order: he is on the point of being sent abroad, which serves to concentrate the mind:

> My dearest Sylvia,
>
> I felt that I must write even though I have seen you so often.
>
> In these last few weeks there have been a lot of occasions when I have felt like having a good old weep, but have kept them back for your sake, I wanted to be brave as you are.
>
> I shall always remember you with a smile on your lips and tears in your eyes, and looking so brave, it was then, as the bus was going that I knew I loved you more than ever.
>
> I felt a proud man, to have a women like you, and when I thought of baby I was indeed a happy husband and a proud father.

Well beloved all I can say now is that God Bless you and baby, and bring me back safe and sound to you both.

Start from to-night dear, and concentrate your thoughts on me, and I shall do likewise, at exactly 10 o'clock every night, and I am sure that though far away, we will, at that moment be very near.

So cheerio my dear, it won't be long before I am with you again for all time so chin up darling the clouds will soon roll by.

With all my love

Sylvia writes on 30 May 1942, apparently not yet having received David's letter:

My dearest David,

I am writing to you again now, though I have my doubts as to whether this letter will reach you. I am sending it to your old address, & shall just hope for the best. I do wish I could get a letter from you – I do miss them, you know darling.

We are all quite O.K. here, but naturally miss you like hell. Ruth makes such a fuss of your photo when she kisses you 'goodnight'. She is also beginning to help say her prayers – she says the last couple of words to each line. It is remarkable how she knows some of the words.

> 'make Root a .... goo gel'
> 'keep her strong .... an' helfy'
> '& please bring daddie .... backy soon'
> '& keep him safe .... an' wayel'

I took Jeff to pictures last night – Friday – to see 'They died with their boots on'. We enjoyed it very much, though we had to queue for a few minutes. I caught sight of the sign opposite the Regal advertising 'Pirelli' tyres, & it took me back some way – remember?

We all went shopping this afternoon – that is, Fay, myself & the three 'kids' (as Ruth calls them). We finished up in the Lyon's for 'ee-cream & Ruth thoroughly enjoyed it. She is a terror though, she does everything the boys do. She won't let me hold her hand, & runs along the road expecting all & sundry to make way for her. She likes to trail her hand along the dirty shop window ledges & you can imagine the state she gets into. She certainly does need restraining, but we must wait until you come home for that. The trouble is she can be so sweet & loving too. When I hold her out at night (& I never forget to give her a kiss for you then) she cuddles up to me & gives me a kiss & murmurs 'nice mummy' – all this while she is soundly sleeping. So how can I really get annoyed with the monkey?

Ralph is off to see Dad on Monday. – We are all very worried about Dad. – Millie has given us a very serious report of what the specialist has said. It is seems it is some disease of the heart, & he must not receive a shock of any sort. Ralph's affair must have upset him, & to ease the effect of when Ralph comes back, Sam (Belle's) is going down on Tuesday for a few days. It will make a rest for Sam too. We don't know what to suggest about Dad – I don't think he knows himself how seriously ill he is.

Well, David my dear, I seem to have no news that I can tell you. We are, naturally, all looking forward to your speedy return, so hurry up & finish the job.

Goodnight darling & God bless you always.—

    Love from Betty and Fay,
        Yours as ever,
        Sylvia.
X from Ruth
X from me.

Managing being apart was not easy. In one letter (14.07.10) Sylvia confesses that although it has been only seven weeks since she last saw David 'it <u>feels</u> like seven years, or seventy'. She goes on to confess:

I find it so difficult to remember what you look like – I keep studying your photographs, & recalling that when you were here I thought they were an excellent likeness, so they must be.

• *On Board the Laconia Off to Reinforce the Troops in North Africa* •

David left in May for the 12,000-mile journey to North Africa. After the shock of the fall of Tobruk, troops were needed to take on Rommel, and David, as a gunner in the 44th Division, along with the 51st Division, was part of those reinforcements.

His ship was the *Laconia*, a requisitioned cruise liner.[1] David did write (07.07.42) but warned that, given the circumstances, this might be the last he could send 'for at least two months', although he hoped 'if it is at all possible' to send a cablegram during the voyage. In the event he did rather better than this.

In this first letter (07.07.42) he describes leaving Bromley and then the sea voyage. This letter is difficult to read in places, since the censor has literally cut out words and, as the letter is double sided, the effect is quite widespread:

We paraded in full marching order, that is carrying everything, and we were really loaded. Then came the usual inspections first the Sgt Majors, then the Troop Commanders, then the C.O. then at 9 o'clock we actually moved, getting to the station at about 9.30, we then entrained and started on our journey at 10.30.

Then they boarded:

We were all leaning over the side watching the land receding from view.
I wonder what all our thoughts were? Mine were very full of mixed emotions, and my thoughts were of you and all that was dear to me.

Even now as I write tears are very near to my eyes, all I can think of now is to get this blasted war over … the sea choppy and very grey, and I have been violently sea sick for one day … this sea sickness is a really rotten feeling, you wish that you had not been born …

Well now for life on board, it is all very boreing, we are over crowded, and have to make our own amusements. The promanard deck is for officers only, and the lower deck is for Sgts., and W.O.s, so we are left the lower deck. The food is good, and an issue three times weekly of fresh fruit is given to everyone … There is a good library, so there is plenty of reading matter, and that suits me very well. Cigs are very cheap paying 3d for ten for Woodbine and 20 for 8d Gold Flake. So living is very cheap. There are about 12 nurses on board here, so competition for their favours amongst the officers is very keen.

The most important thing … is how we sleep … hammocks … so close to-gether, that when the chaps either side of me breath out my hammock con [cut out] when they breath in it expands … for all that I sleep very well.

Facilities for washing and for other things is very good, and everything is spotlessly clean. Water is rationed, but sea water showers are on all day, so there is no need for anyone to be dirty.

P.S. We have no wireless on board, but there is a news sheet printed out and that is the only way in which we are in contact with world events, and it is only a very brief summary of the B.B.C. news. Why I have written this is because I have just read that on 3rd of June London was visited by enemy aircraft but only a few bombs were dropped. I hope dear that everything is O.K. but please look after yourself.

It will be grand seeing land again, even if it only be trees and mud huts … The journey has been peaceful and uneventful for which I suppose we have to thank God.

… Sea, sea and more sea, I did not know there was so much water. We have now travelled over [censored] and are getting into warmer weather, [this last phrase has a pencil line through it and above it is written, in pencil] and the weather is quite warm and the sea is like a pond ... let me tell you my dear, that the sea is grey, and not blue, it is only blue when the sun shines on it, and there is nothing good about it.

Been looking at the snaps I have of you and 'baby', and have been thinking a great deal, it hurts to look at them, and yet I would not be with-out them, it is the world [cut out] baby and I, P.G. will be with you again just us three (for a little while at least.)

In a subsequent letter (16.06.42) he describes the ship as 'over crowded & sweaty ... not a very enjoyable trip at all'. He was, nevertheless, 'feeling fit and excited'; he was 'going to make the best' of what promised to be 'a completely new experience for me', although it was tempered by the fact that 'I had to leave you and baby behind'. To make up for this he promised 'that we are going to have a sea trip to-gether (Please God) after this darn war is over'.

He describes various ways of passing the time: letter writing, reading, playing 'Housey-Housey' and card games, 'interesting lectures' and 'a minature brains trust'. There was 'a sing-song on deck in the cool of the night with a nice breeze ... blowing, a welcome relief from the heat of the day'. The songs were:

all sentimental ditties, 'Old fashioned lady' 'Danny Boy' 'We'll meet again' 'In apple blossom time' 'When they sound the last all clear' and the favourite song 'The white cliffs of Dover'. What thoughts of home they conjour up, and what memories of happier days ... it's nice to ... lose one self in song

He follows the news of the war as best he can and it sounds 'discouraging' and he wonders 'what is really happening, news on the ship is very sketchy'. The letter ends abruptly, however, because someone 'wants to sleep on the table, you see my dear, we sleep and eat in the same place'. He only has time to add 'Sweet dreams and God Bless, give baby a nice big "cuddy" for me'.

Another, very contrasting, story of life on board was given by Ralph en route for India. Sylvia summarises the letter for David (04.08.42). Ralph's cabin was shared with five other sergeants and had a cool-air ventilator set into the wall so that his:

> greatest joy was to strip & stand on a chair in front of this, & move the ventilator so that the cool breeze played all over the body. He can buy, by queuing up at the right time ... Libby's peaches & tinned milk – quite cheap, too. I wonder if you fellows get a fair share of all that's going? or is it snapped up by the officers & N.C.O's?

David's voyage broke off in South Africa and Sylvia subsequently received a letter from a Mr Light (03.07.42), on paper naming him as a director of Salt River Sweets Works Ltd in Cape Town, giving news that 'we had the pleasure of entertaining your beloved husband. He spent a very pleasant evening at our home.'

• *Arriving in Egypt* •

David disembarked on 27 July at Tufic on the Suez Canal and his impressions (01.08.42) were stark; there was:

> nothing romantic about this part of the East with its hovels and brothels, camels and cars, veiled and modern women. The natives live in most terrible ... houses ... [that are] crumbling and derelict ... sleeping and eating with their cattle. There are children in abundance, it seems as if this is the only thing that can be easily produced in this hot sandy country.

Given time his mood shifts, reverting (18.09.43) to his earlier 'great excitement':

> the land of the Pharo's meant to me a new world to see strange people & even stranger customs fascinated me, & I felt greatly privileged to have had a glimpse at this land of bondage, & to-day after 4000 years it is still a land of bondage, but this time it is not Isrial, but to their own people. Cairo I liked, it was continental. I could imagin Paris being very similar, with you I could live quite happily there for the rest of my life.

He describes life 'in the dessert at a base camp', which 'is a lot better than I expected':

Flies and sand are our chief troubles, the food good but gritty, the sand gets to every thing, it swirls about in the wind creating miniture dust storms.

The day starts at 5.30am tea at 6 am, then work, breakfast at 8.45 then next parade at 10am, work till 12, dinner and then next parade is at 4pm. 6.30 supper which is the main meal, then time is yours until lights out.

We have plenty of rest, the reason being that it is to darn hot to work or play.

Egypt is an expensive place for the Tommy the smallest coin being a piastre which is worth 2½d I have just paid 7 piastras for some tooth paste, Beer is 8½ piastres a bottle, so that is too dear to drink. Arab boys keep coming round the tents selling all manor of things, including ices costing about 6d.

Each week David was issued fifty cigarettes, 'which helps to keep expences down' (26.08.42), and each week he also ordered four cans of beer, four tins of fruit, a tin of milk and an additional thirty cigarettes from the NAFFI so that he could be seen 'in the cool of the evening tucking into a tin of peaches and cream, swilling it down with beer, and right enjoyable it is too'. His diet later included grapes, eggs and bananas, with the promise of 'to-morrow [I] shall finish off one grape-fruit & two pomegranits. It was a joy eating the fruits of civilisation' (20.10.42). A wireless allowed them to listen 'to the beautiful chimes of Big Ben (never thought so before)' and he and his fellow soldiers cried 'sentimental tears to croonings of Vera Lyne' (30.09.42).

He was given leave in Cairo, which proved to be (20.08.42):

one of my most weirdest experiences of my life ... Cairo must be the melting pot of the East, Syrians, Greeks, French and I think every nationality of the sun abide here.

Immediately we got there we thought of our tummies, and had three eggs, bacon and chips, coffee fresh rolls and cream butter, it was a great meal.

The two of us then took a two horse carriage to take us to the most interesting parts of Cairo. We saw the King's Palace, but that was disappointing, it was very similar to Buckingham Palace, but what was interesting, was the Blue Mosque, and the modern Mosque close by.

They were both colosal places of worship, the design and structure was really wonderful. It's a strange thing that people will spend thousands of pounds for a place of worship, yet they the people who were created in the image of God live in hovels. I wonder if God demands that, I certainly don't think so.

Then we went through the native Bazzars, and that intrigued me, I can't really explain it, it was one big Petticoat Lane but as ancient as the civilisation of Egypt itself. I shall one day P.G. let you see it for yourself.

Incidently I had my fortune told, the most important thing being, I shall live till 83 years old (can you put up with me that long) and shall only be out here 8½ months, so things sound promising.

Also took photographs of myself, and they are sending them on, I hope.

The rest of the day was spent in walking, eating, and drinking iced drinks and cream, and believe me they turn out some darn good drinks.

The modern women is really beautiful, but they were mainly Syrians and Greeks, the Egyptians you can't see much of, they are dressed in long shapeless black cloth and veiled, so there beauty if any, was not to be seen.

It all went a lot too quickly, but a good time was had by all.

A very important break from the camp occurred when he visited Alexandria (3.09.42) for the Jewish festivals:

There were nigh on a thousand Jews up for the Festival and it was a case of 'Come the four corners of the world.' They represented all the known fighting units of the allies, Army, Navy, and Air Force, and I was very proud to be amongst them. After the fast (note: The Day of Atonement) most of us went along to the Zionist club where food and wine was given us, then a social was held, organised by the Palestinian units in Alex. These Palestinians are a boisterous lot, they know the exzuberance of a youthful nation, virile and healthy, contented and happy, speaking Hebrew and scorning 'Yiddish', and a splendid time they gave us.

David takes space in the letter to reflect (01.08.42) on how much he missed Sylvia; he wanted 'snaps of you and baby as soon as possible' and letters, but not ordinary mail since this 'takes too long', but rather airmail or airgraph, 'even an E.F.M. telegram once so often, it will stop me worrying'. The news of air raids over London explains his urgency.

When the post does arrive (09.08.42):

I keep reading and re-reading those letters of yours, it seemed ages since I had heard from you, and I missed those letters of yours tremendously.

On 30 September 1942 David showed his appreciation of Ruth's drawings that he had received; they:

are getting quite good, her sketch of you was somewhat Epstein fasion, but shows promise. I heartily endorse her own opinion when she says 'clever Roofie.' It's good that you are finding time to go about and seeing West-End shows, it breaks the monotony and drives the blues away and I wish that I had been with her, in the park on Bank Holiday, am looking forward to the future when Bank Holidays will not be spent apart, but be spent pleasantly to-gether (P.G.)

• *Home News: of Mice (in the Bath) and Men (Predatory) Prayers, Photos and Trips to the Park* •

The letters that Sylvia sent are consistent in their concerns and content, as well as in her need to respond to every snippet of news from David. As such she was relieved (16.06.42) to hear from him as he was about to set sail, even if:

> there was not very much news in it, but at least I knew you were well ... I promise to write frequently now that I have your A.P.O. number.

Sylvia also promises, once she has a fixed address, 'to arrange for an overseas newspaper for you. It will keep you in touch with current affairs as far as possible.' She fills David in with news from home, various male relatives home on leave or expected, including his nephew, Lionel, brother Alf and brother-in-law Sam, who was especially looking fit and well, having lost 18lb in weight. Sylvia worries about whether David has received two letters she had written him and urges him to date and number his letters so that she can keep them in order. However, most of her message is of her love:

> Needless to say how very much I have missed you these last few weeks – it has seemed like as many years. It was not just the belief that you had gone, but I have so missed your letters & phone calls ... Do you remember to say goodnight to me still? I still do at the same time but at what time do you now? One thing I am curious about, do you keep to the double summer time which we have here or have you, now that you have left England, judge your time by the sun?

Sylvia turns to Ruth, who:

> is always asking after you. Her first words when she awoke yesterday morning were 'Mummy, – daddy here!' – I presume that she must have been dreaming very vividly about you, & you were her first thought on waking. And then, of course, I found your letter waiting. Ruth insisted on holding a page of it too while I was reading it. – I shall ask her to

draw a page of her famous 'gah gahs' for you, & shall enclose it – though I hope the censors won't think it some sort of code – she does such weird shapes sometimes.

A trip to the park and its swimming pool provoked a special sadness:

> You always said you would teach her to swim by the time she was two – but then, who knew there would be a war? I was a trifle upset because you were not there to take her in for her first dip, but we shall wait for you to teach her to dive off the top board & to go down the chute.

Sylvia ends:

> As for me, David, well you know exactly how I feel. I once said that you knew more about me than I knew about myself. But please don't worry about me; as long as you look after yourself, I shall be O.K.
>
> God bless you, darling, & send you home soon.
>
> All my dearest love,
>
> Yours as ever,
>
> Sylvia.
> X from me
> X from Ruth

A letter a week later (23.06.42) continues these themes, along with frustration at still not having heard from David and news of his father:

> being laid up the past few days with a very severe attack of lumbago. It rather worried Ruth to see him in bed, & she kept saying 'Shoes on getup – lazy Gumpne'.

There is the tale of Ruth's inoculations:

The first test was rather a painful one – an injection into each arm. Poor Ruth – she didn't <u>scream</u> for a few seconds like the other youngsters, but she cried so pathetically all the way along the road going home.

Sylvia's depiction of wartime life (20.12.42) illustrates how even one as young as Ruth accepted the dramas of war. When arguing with cousin Tony over a toy, and told by him:

's'my house'... she answers with equal indignation 'I live here.' She continues, & explains herself. 'My house bombed out – what I do? – got no house? live here.'

There were other demands and complications. Sylvia's old boss was having problems finding staff (01.09.42) and asked if she could go back to work for him, even if only for six hours a week. She writes: 'I worried so much over that letter, but how could I do it', since it would mean four hours travelling and she was also needed at home. 'I have taken over the cooking here, Fay spends the entire day in the shop.'

Sylvia felt she had to say no:

but it is nice to have some one to think highly of you (you do too, of course, darling.) – If it weren't for the journey, I'd feel so tempted.

Then she received a letter from the district valuer (22.09.42) following up the claim for the household goods destroyed when they were bombed, a painful reminder of their 'home together some way back in the distant past'. The strain was not just on her; in the same letter she refers to a friend who:

seems greyer than ever, & so much older & more lined. But then, most parents seem to be showing the signs of the strain after having family life broken up by this blasted war which has already lasted three long years – and, for all we know, may last another three more.

At other times (08.09.42) Sylvia's mood was very different; for example the humour in her tale of 'the calamity of a mouse in the bath ...':

When I removed the cover to run in the hot water, there it was, stretched out. As you know, I don't worry about live mice, but dead ones make me feel ill. Question was, how to remove the body? Betty said she would do it (after lengthy persuasion) but she wanted to finish her letter to Ralph first. I could, of course, have postponed my bath until tomorrow night, but since we have started our economising in fuel, we switched off the heater & only turn it on for baths, & washing day etc. And so, having had the electricity running for a couple of hours, I can't of course waste it. By the way, didn't I once fill the bath for you & afterwards found a mouse in it too? Ah me, may such be the greatest worry of my life.

The mice were certainly persistent. Three months later (13.12.42) the house was 'being over run'. Traps were set – two dozen in total – which caught:

eight of the blighters – five in the shop, & three in the scullery … catching mice wholesale is some sort of training for what you are doing, really – only you are catching bigger rats.

Sylvia describes the start of sweet rationing (28.07.42), which caught her by surprise. It was 2oz per person per week, and people were allowed to buy a whole month's supply at one time. The amount 'is small, but not too bad really'. She notices how:

all the shops had such beautiful displays of sweets & chocolates & … Woolworth's had a whole counter show. The lack of long queues that up till now have collected as soon as a sweet comes into view makes it just like pre-war days.

Other deprivations were noticed approaching Christmas. Visiting a store, Jeffrey was 'disgusted' by Father Christmas, 'an old man, very little, & with only a few teeth – not at all the portly figure of bygone years'. Sylvia had to explain that because Father Christmas had also been called up this was 'Grand father Xmas' (07.12.42).

The local park comes up:

with the idea of encouraging stay at home holidays, introduced a band – from 7.30 to 9.30, – Not on Sundays though, that would be lowering the tone of the district.

Sylvia got to see the first night of Richard Tauber in *Land of Smiles* (28.07.42):

> It was a very good show, & the singing was truly beautiful. Tauber had to give four encores for 'You are my hearts delight', & he also gave a short speech at the close of the performance – being the opening night. I thoroughly enjoyed it, though it was a little on my conscience at having left Ruth – The only occasions I have left her like that has been when you have been on leave. – I didn't get home until so awfully late too, & Doris was lying in bed reading to her, & optimistically expecting her to go to sleep.

Sylvia gave up on knitting and instead joined a lending library (21.07.42):

> When the girl issued me with a number, she asked if she should make it out as Mr. & Mrs. in case my husband should need a book. – I just said I didn't think you would be needing one from them for quite a while yet.

Sylvia chose a novel based on the period just prior to Munich, which took an American, anti-Russian, point of view. The author was a 'definite Right winger [which] is partly spoiling the book for me'.

Sylvia went to the cinema (18.08.42) but this was not without its hazards. Walking back that evening, along a road dark with the blackout:

> I was thinking of you so much. I could almost imagine you were with me, my thoughts were so real. Then into my most pleasant reverie, a male voice said 'Goodnight'. It was pitch dark, but the person was evidently walking the opposite way. When I crossed the road, someone else accosted me. I could just discern a forage cap, but he seemed such a kid. – It was almost pathetic. – He suggested that I stay out a while longer, but I'm afraid I must have disarmed him when I said that my baby might be crying. He just said oh! & lagged behind. He did follow at a discreet distance just to make sure that I was only going as far as I said. Next time I shall say I can't stay out as

I have my <u>son</u> home on leave. – The cheek of it. – I might have been fair, fat & forty, but as long as it was some one in skirts. – Were you as bad as that when you were in England? A uniform does get away with a lot, it's true.

A more obvious danger were the air raids, preceded by air-raid warnings. These are mostly alerts during the daytime involving 'no activity' (28.07.42); nevertheless, the previous night was:

> very hefty, & I was rather glad Ruth was in bed with me. One terrific bout of gunfire disturbed her & she said 'Nasty warning – goo-way' ('narsy,' she says). She was busy telling everyone all about it this morning, & was most indignant at having been disturbed. She doesn't realise that little over a year ago a whole house nearly collapsed on her when she was asleep, & she didn't even turn a hair. – Anyway darling, don't worry about us here, we're all able to take care of ourselves (I hope) as long as you look after yourself.

So Ruth, an increasingly 'independent little monkey' (15.09.42), was a constant source of stories and these were sufficiently detailed that David could see her development and share the parental pride. A typical example is when Sylvia encloses a page of her drawings (28.07.42), which 'seem extra good to me this time … it really is clever for a mite of barely two'. They acquired a new cat, 'a tiny black fluffy thing' that Ruth 'speaks to in an extra gentle voice, & almost croons over it'. Ruth learnt to put on her own socks and 'was so pleased about it. "Clever girl" she said, "Write—" but I raced her to it, "Write tell daddy?" we said together. – She was so amused that we should both have thought of it together.'

In the same letter Sylvia takes care to give news of other family members. Lionel was in New Brunswick, Canada and his descriptions of the ice cream sundaes in drug stores 'certainly made my mouth water', while 'the bread is so white, he says it melts in his mouth'. Both Alf and Sam were home on weekend leave, Alf looking 'fit and well' and Sam 'too seemed very smart'. Sylvia does not say but surely she felt the contrast with how much easier their army lives seemed compared to David's.

David had certainly picked up on something of the mood when he checked with Sylvia (16.06.42) as to whether 'you are also on real good terms with Fay again, it really upset me to see you both on such indifferent terms'.

Sylvia was busy finding alternative ways of keeping David's presence alive in the family rituals and routines. Visiting the cemetery before the High Holy Days, she tells David that she 'paid your respects, & put in a silent prayer for you too' (01.09.42). There were prayers at home (21.07.42):

> when I put Ruth to bed tonight she had said her prayers, she asked for your 'photo – 'Talkit, daddy.' – I gave it to her & she held it lovingly in two hands & mumbled to it. – during the mumbling she said 'Miss you daddy' & carried on with her muttering. Then made me 'talkit daddy.' – I said 'God bless you, & please come back soon' – & she chimed in 'big boat, – Rootie doggie, & a bike, like Tony's, & a weeny baby' – & I had to repeat each of the items to you for her. Talk about a dictatorship – But she didn't ask you for them, I had to do it for her. Can't you send her home a camel or something we can keep in the back yard?

Another technique to preserve David's memory in his daughter was Ruth's dinner plate with the alphabet on the rim, from which she could:

> pick out 'D – daddy'. She sometimes has to turn the plate around two or three times before she can find it, but she does find it eventually.

Keeping the connection going was urgent as Ruth's grasp on this figure of 'daddy' could be painfully elusive. Sylvia tells (04.08.42) how:

> she can most times pick you out on that group 'photo of your regiment. When she hesitates, I guide her by saying, 'Look for his face – it's a nice face.' And when she guesses at one she queries 'This a nice face?' Coming home through the park she saw a 'sojer', (as she now calls them) & she asked 'Nice face? – daddy?' I agreed, 'yes, nice face, but it's not daddy.' So she said, 'Like it, this one?' 'Not too bad.' I said, 'yes.' 'Take it home' she said quickly, 'buy Roofie bike, wow-wow, baby' etc etc. It seems anyone will do for a daddy as long as she gets her list of requirements. But she does know her real daddy, because when she suggests that any particular 'sojar' is daddy she follows up with 'but not mummy's Dave.'

Sylvia also had photos, of course, and she appreciated (29.09.42) the album of polyfotos – forty-eight separate photos during which the sitter could move their head freely and so provide a series of quite natural rather than posed portraits. She looked at each picture in turn:

> I am now on number five of your photographs; – it is already the fifth week you know. It is rather a nice one, too, though I don't fancy the next one – that is where you are making such a peculiar face, I do hope you will be home before I get to the end of the sheet, though of course I can always start again, but I'd rather you were back before then.

She also wore what Ruth called '"Daddy's 'jamas?" – They are very warm, & somehow seem to bring you closer to me'.

On 7 July 1942 Sylvia continued to write, but still without having heard from David. She describes a sister-in-law, Marie, giving her:

> a winter coat & leggings for Ruth. It is a really lovely set in blue, with velvet collar & pocket flaps. – Ruth is so proud of it – she wouldn't take it off when I tried it on her. But, oh Davie, she looks so much older – she isn't really a baby any longer. – The years are slipping away, & we are simply wasting them apart. – There will be such a lot of time to make up for when this is damn war is over, – so please, darling, hurry up & come home – & all in one piece, too!

Then she writes:

> I wonder, David whether something can be arranged. – Every time we see a very young baby, Ruth says 'Root some o' that.' I told her we should have to wait until daddy comes home as he has all the pennies, but she is so impatient. – So you see, darling, another very good reason why you should hurry home.

A joking reference, but this hope for a new child is a theme that both of them returned to in the years ahead, and it would be 1947 before that wish was fulfilled.

Sylvia found comfort (28.07.42) from a MOI (Ministry of Information) film called *Troopship*, which follows the life of the soldiers on board from the time of embarkation until they land some two months later. They are shown eating, at PT (Physical Training), even washing their 'smalls', and she wonders:

> Do you also use your knee as a washing board? … I looked eagerly for you among the crowd, but naturally could not find you … this left me very weepy, but it is surprising how awfully sentimental I have become.

When a card does not arrive on her birthday she looks at the one David sent the previous year and 'I console myself with that' (11.08.42), and in the same letter she talks of some maps that he had brought home, one showing Europe and the west coastline of Africa as far east as Libya:

> I followed an imaginary journey for you as far as the Cape, but couldn't go further east. Now, of course, I can't place you again if you are somewhere in Egypt, so will you please see what you can do with regards pushing Rommel out of Libya & then I can once again follow your activities.

She was also concerned about his other possible activities, checking whether during his leave in Cairo he 'painted the town very red … Don't forget to bring Ruth a baby brother – but not a black one' (18.08.42).

David sought to reassure her (26.08.42): 'am still a clean boy. "I ain't misbehaving but saving my love for you."' Sylvia, however, remained cautious (20.10.42); she was 'pleased to note that you are "still a clean boy"', but wondered whether, having met up with an old friend, David had now received 'a few tips, & also some recommended addresses'. She ends: 'Anyway darling, we discussed that little problem before you went away, & I think you knew my views.'

Other worries dominated, however, with the news from the media. 'The papers quote "great days ahead" for you fellows, & I don't know quite how that is meant' (27.08.42) and then the nine o'clock news bulletin reported renewed fighting in Egypt (01.09.42):

> I try not to imagine to what extent you, personally, may be involved, but not having a letter from you for some time it is rather worrying.

Then she reports (12.11.42) how she is:

> still anxiously watching the papers for news of the battle area … The news
> is quite full of hope, & everyone is optimistic – very nice too, when we are
> here & you are out there, in the thick of it.

In her last letter of the year (31.12.42) she asks if David remembers an
old neighbour, prompting him 'of course you do – we met her once in
the High Rd while you were on leave'. At that time she had been proud
of her husband's promotion to petty officer. Then Sylvia adds, 'I have just
heard that he has been killed – it rather upset me, I'm afraid.'

• *David: 'Under The Desert Stars' And 'Rough Times': The Battle of El Alamein* •

Returning to David, he felt the absence from home, especially because
Sylvia's birthday 'has now come and gone, and very sorry I am that I was
not there to spend it with you', although he had sent her a cablegram
which he hoped she got in time. In the meantime, he had been 'sleeping
under the Desert stars, we were all on a small training stint', and he notes
(06.09.42) that 'If you are of a poetical nature, there is a certain beauty
about the dessert'.

These letters also provide a moment to move from his immediate family
feelings to connect with why he was in a soldier's uniform (09.08.1942):

> I love you a lot, and believe me I am not fighting just because I believe in
> King or country, but because I want to give you and baby a place in the sun,
> under fascism me and mine would be doomed.

The meaning behind these words, the reality of war, now takes shape
when he writes (18.09.43) of the:

> wastes of the desert, with its sand storms, flies, 'gypo guts' & dysentery,
> nothing but a glowing sun on never ending stretches of sand, the devil

himself could not of improved on the place, in such a place we did our three weeks training for the battles ahead.

Then the training turns into the real thing:

By night we travelled into the 'Blue' that is what we called the desert where fighting was taking place & that was Alamein, I was not worried, perhaps it was best, it was a case of 'Ignorance is bliss', it turned out that our first positions were to be second line defence & out of range of enemy fire, all to the good, though the flies were still very much in range, they drove us on the verge of madness.

Perhaps to illustrate better what the flies were like, I'll put it this way, if you put a cup of tea down for one moment, at least a dozen of the beggars would be in there helping you to drink it.

The evenings were grand, nothing then worried you a cool breeze would blow, the Earth was still, the sky took on some glorious hues, I have never seen a more beautiful sunset than that over the desert, a beautiful ending to a day of sorrow.

Aug. 30th 1942 Sunday, a day as long as I live I shall never forget its horrors, it even chills me now when I think about it.

We were now prepared to go forward Sunday Aug. 30th at about 10 o'clock pm we were taking over gun positions from New Zealanders in a forward area, it so happened that at precisely at the same moment Rommel made his push. Well it was our baptism of fire, for four hours we were shelled heavy & small stuff was slung at us from all directions, we could do nothing more than lay on our bellies till it abated.

Believe me sweetheart I said every prayer that my childhood memories brought to my mind.

I came through O.K. but we lost two killed & 12 wounded I then knew what war was & I was a very sober sort of person.

We were in action, one week in the New Zealand Box another in the Qattara depression, & so we shifted from North to south along the Alemien line, we shelled they returned the compliment, Stukas came bombed and went, it was static till the 23rd Oct.

Great preparations were being made, gun pits were being dug, & ammunition was pilling up, six hundred rounds per gun, & we were busy, sweat & toil was our lot, but we were keen, excited, the plan of attack could not fail.

Oct. 23rd Zero hr 9'0'clock p.m. we were ready a shell up the barrel, the breach closed & No 3 had his hand on the firing lever, soon the greatest barrage this war was to know would soon open up.

What thoughts you have, the suspence of waiting is really terrible, your nerves are on edge, you dare not speak, because you would only betray your fears & at all cost you must hide them from your friends, the whistle blew – what a relief, you forgot everything, with monotonous regularity flash & bang blots out any thing in your mind.

The battle is on, fire & destruction is paving a way for the infantry's advance, early morning finds us dead tired but all objectives won ten days after Jerry is on the run. Ten days that shook Rommel & gave England a new heart.

Well with that ended my fighting, the next phase was Mareth, & that sweetheart will be another letter.[2]

David, in the midst of all this, was finding it difficult to write home. A letter dated 4 November 1942 (which Sylvia did not receive until 7 December 1942) simply notes:

Please don't worry if news from me is very scanty and slow, but you must know by now that the battle for North Africa is on, and is going great guns for us, The papers will be giving you most of the dope, and believe me, we are pushing ahead as fast as the Italians & Germans can run, its grand news, and the moral of us lads is at the top of its form, so you folks

at home, can see to it that the home fires are burning bright for when P.G.
we get home.

He tries to be ordinary, telling of a letter from his brother-in-law Lou,
then he moves on to his love:

> Well dearest one, still missing you a hell of a lot … there is no truth in the
> old adage out of sight, out of mind, to me it is still 'absence makes the heart
> grow fonder'.

He is positive:

> Never mind, the time is drawing very near to the time, when we shall be
> together again, and think only of this period of parting as a bad dream. I
> am going to be hopelessly out of date with my love making, but with your
> help, our second honeymoon ought to be a pleasant one.

He also gives some further news of the battle (10.11.42):

> it seems that all England is ringing joy bells for our great Victory out here. I
> who was in it could hardly believe that it was achieved in such short a time.

> You should see the lads out here, happy and proud, and Nov. 5th was a real
> Guy Fawkes day in every sence.

> The German War machine will soon break up, and hope to be seeing you
> sooner than I expected.

> During the time I have been out here, I have had some pretty rough times,
> but Thank God, I had you to pray hard for me, it must of helped, for here
> I am safe & sound, waiting for the time when I get on that 'big boat' of
> Ruthies' straight to blighties shore.

> You would have been amused when news of the victory came over the air,
> at the chaps singing that song, 'Little man, you've had a busy day' especially
> that part 'put away that gun, the war is over for to night.'

• *In and Out of Hospital – and 1942 Draws to an End* •

The effect of 'the rough times' was such that David ended the year in quite a different place. On 13 November 1942 (although he gives the date as 1939) he writes, 'lying in bed, between two white sheets in hospital in Alex suffering from tonsilitus'. He assures Sylvia that there is 'nothing to be alarmed about'. It was not the diphtheria they first feared, but more a bad throat, and he admits, 'I am just run down, and this rest and attention will do me good'. Now safely away from the battle, he was able to allude, using humour to sweeten the effect, to the pressures that brought him to this point of collapse:

> The most annoying part about every thing is I stuck three months of Desert warfare dodging shells and Stuka bombs, living in slit trenches three foot deep, eating bully beef and little else, and now that we were going to have a cushy time of it, I get ill.

> Still this hospital is a very nice place, right on the sea front, the food good.

> This is my first day here, and I had a real hot bath, I was really dizzy after it, it was I presume a shock to the system as it was the first bath I had for at least three months.

David then says that his 'only worry is your mail', because 'it will take a hell of a time catching up with me'. He advises Sylvia to keep writing to him so either they will forward it on or else 'when I reach the 58th Field Reg. I shall have a nice stack of mail waiting for me'. He takes time to comment on the war, sustaining a spirit of optimism: 'News all along the war fronts still continues to be good, with a bit of luck, the war should be over early next year, at least I think so. Roll on 1943 its going to be victory year.'

By November David was out of hospital, telling Sylvia that he was fully recovered and, while waiting to rejoin his regiment and catch up on his mail, he was 'spending a pleasant time in Alex, eating of the best, and doing myself well'. Again he is optimistic about the war:

things are still going great out here, in a short time North Africa should be clear of all enemy troops … I can't see how the war is going to last too long, Russia, like us is proving to the world, that Germany can be beat on land, as well as on the sea. Italy must be by now very much on the breaking point, and she won't last very long.

Even while he knows that some of the troops might be going back into battle:

I hope I am one of the lucky ones to be sent back to blighty … it is a hell of a long time since I last saw you, and I am beginning to miss you & baby tremendously.

This anxiety is very strong. He insists (10.12.42) that he will write to Sylvia as often as possible, three to four times a week, 'knowing the concern you have for my safety', and there was catching up with family to be done, brother-in-law Ralph serving in India, brother Alf still in England 'and looking well. It must be a consolation to Mother to have one of her son's at home & out of trouble.'[3]

• *Sylvia: Feeling 'The Odd One'* •

For all of David's concerns for Sylvia, he caused her great pain when (08.12.42) she happened on a letter he had sent to Lou, who had then left it 'propped up on the mantelpiece for anyone to read'. It bore the instruction, 'Don't tell Sylvia or Mother'. She comments:

Perhaps you were right – why should I be told? I ought, by now be used to being left out of things. There was the time when Sam's niece, Mary, got married – only I was excluded not that any of the family went, but an invitation was sent to them all. And when Lou & Doris went over to Eva I was carefully not told, but Alf casually mentioned it. – And when Lou & Doris went up West with Betty & Sam recently, I was again kept in the dark. This must sound like a moan – it isn't really – it's just that I felt very hurt that you too should say – 'Don't tell Sylvia!'

Sorry, now, that I've written all this, but I'm glad to have got it off my chest. Trouble is, I suppose, that I won't realise that I am an odd one – not having my husband to partner me – & with the added 'entanglement' of a child. – I shouldn't complain – Ruth & I have spent some truly exciting weekends in the Park.

Sylvia moves quickly to more details of Ruth's life, for example, when cousin Jeffery told her that fairies do not exist and are just 'fairy tales', she replied indignantly, 'Fairies haven't got <u>tails</u> – they've got <u>wings</u>'. Then Sylvia ends: 'Sorry if part of this has been a telling off – I am rather foolish, I know'

Then the approaching Christmas and accompanying celebrations allow her (13.12.42) to be mellower in mood:

I shall miss not having you near at hand, the start of a new year has always meant such a lot to us. I sincerely hope that this coming one will see the answer to all my prayers.

It was also an opportunity to reminisce, specifically in response to David wondering how they might have changed over the last period. She reassures him (14.12.42) that:

I have not changed much since you left, still not a grey hair – I thought I'd have found hundreds by now after worrying about you and your antics in Egypt. Still, as it's only Jerry you're chasing & not nurses or ATS, I shouldn't really be too concerned. Ruth, as you say, has grown tremendously since you went away. After all, she is getting on for three now & the past few months have seen such an enormous change in her. She talks very well & is most sensible in her ways too. She is always talking about 'when my daddy comes home', & she has made such a lot of plans for the future. She is always adding to that long, long list of things she intends having; – as a matter of fact, I too have a nice little list, but I dare not mention them here. You hurry home, then please God we can work it out between us.

In her New Year's Eve letter (31.12.42) Sylvia describes seeing a film where one of the characters is asked about 'love':

She, with stars in her eyes, says 'Sometimes you wake up in the night – you hear him breathing at your side, & you whisper a fervent prayer "Dear God – please take <u>me</u> first."' Everyone laughed, but it was so true that I felt more like crying. I have often thought something similar – I couldn't bear it if anything happened to you. So please darling, do take care of yourself, for both our sakes.

Then:

Big Ben has just chimed midnight, & I have been in to see Ruth. – She was sound asleep, so I kissed her goodnight & your photo too. – So the three of us were together, even if only in my mind. – This is the third new year Ruth has seen come in – & each of them without you. – Please try to be here when this one goes out.

In retrospect we know that the war, and David's part in it, is far from over. Remembering David's letter (10.12.42) where he talked of how '[I]t must be a consolation to Mother to have one of her son's at home & out of trouble', we are aware, as 1942 comes to an end, that her other son, David, is far from 'out of trouble'.

....

Notes

1 This ship subsequently became famous when, on 12 September 1942, it was sunk off the coast of West Africa by a German U-boat. Its commander launched a rescue mission when he realised that many of the 3,000 passengers were civilians, including women and children, and Italian prisoners of war.

2 The powerful impact of the mortar attack is supported by other accounts. 'As the troops passed over the ground the next day, they saw how much destruction has been wrought on the Germans: "Whole gun crews," writes one man, "were lying dead round their guns. Even in the slit trenches and dug-outs many had been killed."' (MOI, undated, pp.77–8). The onslaught

was not just one-sided, there was the fear induced by the dive-bombing German Stukas: 'the very embodiment of Blitzkreig, terrifying with its fitted siren that shrieked your doom as it fell out of the sky in a near-vertical dive' (Bierman & Smith, 2002, p.69). Another soldier wrote of the horror of dysentery and dust storms, of the temperatures that could drop from 40°C by day to 0°C at night. A soldier's tin hat 'came in handy … as a shovel, a cooking pot, a toilet and a wash basin'. The bully beef was a staple diet which was eaten at night 'when it was cold and not too greasy' (Bierman & Smith, 2002, pp.81–2).

A fuller description of what it was like to be 'a gunner' can be taken from an account of a mortar team on a training exercise. It is a different army, the American, and a later war, Korea, but the experience is surely similar. The writer is awed by:

> the neat meshing of teamwork, speed, subtlety of reflex, and mechanical skill. Rather like an athletic ballet with men in almost synchronous motion, all leading up to the final, gratifying, earth-jolting *crump-crump* when, a mile away, the shells land. And this is still peace time practice – not without dangers, of shells falling short and killing the wrong people or for a mortar to burst apart while being loaded. And in war time, well, it was never so neat and pretty in combat
>
> (Styron, 2010, pp.95–6)

3   In their account of the war in North Africa, Bierman and Smith (2002) acknowledge that this 'was a bitter and implacable war in which death came in many terrible ways' (p.1), but they add that this battle took place 'without hate … virtually without atrocities … Conducted across a largely unpopulated terrain, it provided no scope for the slaughter of non-combatants, intended or inadvertent' (p.2).

Three

1943
THE RIDDLE OF SEX AND OTHER QUESTIONS

THE YEAR 1943 STARTS with David using a quiet time after the battle to describe the detail of daily life and ponder over the way the war was progressing and how it could progress. Sylvia describes her own part in the war effort, and that of other family members, as well as the sadness of seeing and sorting what had been stored of their belongings that had been retrieved from their bombed home. There is discussion of anniversaries, of weddings, of May Day, of the Jewish Passover. There are some honest and painful discussions about managing the sexual tensions of being apart. Within this is news of battles, David 'in the thick of things' at the battles on the Mareth Line, Wadi Akarit and the fall of Sousse, then Tunis and Bizerta and finally Operation Husky, the invasion of Sicily. The year ends with David getting leave and excitedly heading for home.

• David: Sitting Pretty, Thinking Politically •

The year starts (17.01.43) with David:

> in the wilds of North Africa some where, enjoying a nice spell of spring weather … We are still doing nothing to help the war effort just sitting pretty, not that I am worried, I think I have seen enough action to last me a life time.

He had some 'nasty boils' on his neck and finger, but:

> the lads have no sympathy at all, if the boil is on the arm, they
> tell you to cut the arm off, if the neck, they suggest taking the
> head off.

Consequently he was determined that 'when I get home P.G. even if I
have a little pimple I'm going to howl my head off' (17.01.43).

As for the weather:

> after being really grand has broken & the rains have come, its pouring
> heavens hard, & the tent is leaking terribly. Its one of the hardships we have
> got to endure for freedom & democracy, it will be nice to get back to civvy
> street, if only to have four solid brick walls around you.

Other creature comforts come from (20.01.43):

> the pure socialism of the barter system with the natives ... we give them
> tea, sugar & they in turn give us eggs & tomatoes, it seems to be working
> quite well.

Language was a problem; 'tea & sugar like love speaks all languages', but it
could not go much further since (14.02.43):

> the opportunity of mixing freely with the population has not occurred,
> & as usual you pick up the swear words first ... people themselves are
> intelligent but dirty, you never see them without either their Ass or Camel
> ... their women you never see in towns, they certainly keep them well out
> of sight.

David had the occasional 'Divi breaks' and 'while it's nice having this
time off, but the problem is how to spend it'. Sleeping was the option
favoured by many of his comrades, but he preferred catching up with his
mail (20.02.43). In a separate letter, but dated the same day, he reflects on
the war. He retains his habitual, overall optimism:

looking at everything from events that are happening on all fronts, I don't think we can despare, we are definitely winning … this war is in the bag for us, one big Spring offensive on all fronts should see the end of this war by August.

When there was a pause in the advance he explains it as 'we are travelling down hill, but now & again the brakes have to be applied' (20.02.43). David was not just thinking strictly in military terms (14.02.43):

If we could organise all the forces of discontent inside German occupied countries, including also that of Germany, I think this war will finish in a very short time. There is another point of view to take, that is the German people themselves, you can't keep up the morale of the people, when you are losing on all fronts. Hitler has built up his system on a winning cause & the promise of loot & gain of rich subordinate countries, the German people must realise that with the allies on the offensive & successful at that, that promise is lost & gone forever. That in itself might cause in the near future an internal collapse, ecomicaly or otherwise in Germany.

• *Sylvia: 'The Proverbial Elephant Who Never Forgets'* •

Sylvia, meanwhile, was following and commenting on the progress of the war (09.01.43):

Well, darling, the position in North Africa seems rather at a standstill. I daresay the weather is a hindrance to any major advance   but you say in your letter, that by the time I receive it, the position should be well in hand. – We must all be patient though – it is only that after such a rapid advance at the beginning of the offensive, we may have been buoyed up to expect the complete extermination of the Afrika Korps – one, two, three! But now, with the Russian offensive on all sides doing so remarkably well, I find it even more disconcerting to listen to our local critics.

Their little girl was also playing her part in the war effort (16.02.43):

When Ruth eats a slice of bread, she likes it cut into strips & arranged to form a soldier-boy. Now, though, we call it Ronald (Rommel) & of course the quicker Ruth gobbles up his legs, then his hands, & then the rest of him, the sooner Daddy can catch him, & then the sooner Daddy can come home. – Anyway the gag usually works, & we have disposed of the arch villain several times already, so what about coming home?

Sylvia continued to remind David of family life. She describes (03.01.43) the relief of 'News at last from Alfie', no date or detail of where his letter had been sent from, just that he was on 'a little voyage' and headed 'for a sub-tropical climate. – so now of course everyone here is speculating.' Nearer to home, the 'two "lobosses"', Tony and Jeffrey, had been 'surreptitiously looking' and 'giggling' at pictures in an American film magazine showing 'various unknowns in states of dress, semi-undress, etc.' Sylvia had found Ruth:

studying one page very intently, & glancing over her shoulder I read 'The Riddle of Sex'. Further details were 'the truth revealed' – 'stop worrying' – 'write for this marvellous book – only $1.98' etc. etc. – So you see, darling, we needn't worry about her – She'll find out for herself all she needs to know. – This modern generation – they certainly do want to learn young.

Other stories about Ruth include her excitement (07.01.43) about a forthcoming pantomime, *Babes in the Wood*, although Sylvia was shocked by the price of the ticket, '2/6 – can you beat that?'

Two days later (09.01.43) she tells of how:

Ruth woke up one night after I had been in bed about an hour, & wanted 'to be 'scused'. I then asked her if she wanted to come into mummy's bed – you should have seen her scramble in before I changed my mind. She seemed puzzled though, as I have never asked her before – she usually worries me for some time before I give way. – I told her that I couldn't sleep, & she cuddled up & said 'I'll look after you, Mummy – go sleep. – All better now?' – Yesterday I bought some Phosferine tablets – they are a good tonic. I had to explain, of course, what they were for to Ruth. A little regretfully she said 'You won't want me in your bed now.' …

We heard a new song over the wireless – 'Don't do it, – darling!' Ruth was awfully amused; the boys too. 'Who is <u>my</u> darling?' I asked her – 'Daddy', she said. 'Oh, & who is <u>your</u> darling?' I replied – 'Daddy'a well.' 'But who is Daddy's darling?' 'Mummy <u>and</u> Ruthie' she insisted. – Out of the mouths of babes & sucklings —

Keep writing sweetheart darling – & keep cheerful. As Ruth tells me, 'Chins up like daddy says.'

Subsequently she writes: 'your baby is almost three years old? She was only seven months when you went into the army – almost the whole of her lifetime till now' (04.02.44). David clearly appreciates this; writing back in November 1942, although the letter was not received by Sylvia until 20 February 1943, he notes: 'You know dear, your letters re. my little daughter is so entertaining & complete, that she is no stranger to me.' Sylvia describes her need to 'get sentimental' (16.01.43):

Vera Lynn singing on the air this evening, 'When the lights go on again – all over the World'. Ruth was a little puzzled by 'the lights', – & I explained to her that before she was born, there used to be lights in the streets, & no blackout. And when the War is over, the lights will go on again. 'Yes,' she agreed, '& my daddy will come home again.' – 'Where is your daddy?' Jeff asked her. As if explaining to a very tiny child, she told him 'My daddy went on a big boat now, he's in Ee-jit.' Then Fay said, 'What will you do when your daddy comes home?' – & in a sing-song voice that seemed to relish each word, she said 'I'll climb on him – & cuddie him – & give him three big kisses.' – How does that prospect strike you? But you had better hurry up, or else she'll be far too big for that kind of thing. In a little over two months, she'll be three, & we shall have been married six whole years. – I think, maybe, the first half of this period was happier than the second – in spite of Ruth.

Sylvia reminisces that seagulls in the local park remind her of 'those good old days at Torquay' (24.01.43) and hearing the song *Somewhere over the Rainbow* takes her 'back through the years to the last film we saw before Ruth was born – remember?' She describes herself as 'the proverbial elephant who never forgets' (21.01.43) and then (18.02.43) her little daughter joins in:

> Ruth asked me today to tell her a story – 'About when we had a shop 's wel.' It's ages, too, since I told her of those long ago happy days. Now she says 'Please God we'll have a shop – for us – when daddy comes home.' Got very excited when I explained that she could help also. – Hurry up home, darling.

David's memory was, in his turn, prompted by a photo he received (23.12.42) of his mother, Sylvia and Ruth, 'the three women in my life', but with a special emphasis on Sylvia:

> honestly dear I can't enfuse enough about it. You look glamorous, the dress you are wearing I remember very well, as also the ornament you are wearing on it.

Sylvia's letters refer to the wider family (09.01.43). Lionel was using some leave to tour round Canada with some friends and he was 'having the time of his life'; a sharp contrast to 'the kind of life Ralph is leading, & the existence you have, & goodness knows what Alfie is going through'. Sylvia arranged a visit to catch up with Belle (her sister) whose daughter Valerie was home for a few weeks; there was a 'bachelor' party of a friend of the family and then news that Ruth had:

> another of her colds which means , apart from a couple of outings we haven't put our noses outside the door. – This fact, coinciding with Jeff's holiday from school, has proved most tragic. – Still, I suppose there are worse troubles at sea – but not very many, I bet.

• *Sylvia: The Strains of the Home Front* •

There was, then, an underlying strain, so while a visit from Bunty (another niece) was good in that 'Ruth likes her very much, & treats her like an old pal' (05.01.43), it entailed a visit to 'Mother's for lunch' and 'these days, that is more of a problem than it sounds'.

There were also the wider struggles (19.01.43) of wartime life:

I hope you haven't been too worried by the couple of air raids London has recently experienced. We are all O.K. The barrage put up was truly terrific, though a trifle un-nerving. The alert during the evening found Ruth & Jeff still awake, & although it meant rousing Tony, Fay & I decided to bring them all down. They behaved very well, & soon settled down to draughts, Ludo & Snaky Ladders. After an early all clear, we packed them all off to bed again. The second alert, in the early hours of the morning – found Ruth sound asleep, & I hadn't the heart to disturb her, so we stayed put. Fay & Betty came down again with the children, & poor old Jeff was worried in case the Hippodrome was blitzed. (As I mentioned in one of my previous letters, we have seats for the pantomime for Saturday.) He was also rather concerned about his teacher – she had intended teaching them the eight times table the following morning, & now, with this disturbance of her sleep, maybe she would be feeling too tired to do so. (She wasn't thank goodness, & Jeff now proudly recites 8x1 etc. without a single error).

A subsequent letter (25.04.43) touches on this same issue, presenting a humourous aspect to what must have been a most scary time:

We had an alert recently & as Fay was still in her bath Betty went upstairs to bring the boys down to put them into my bed. Jeff was half dazed & having put his dressing gown on for himself she gave him his slippers to put on himself while she roused Tony. Imagine our amusement when we found him with his slippers on his head & him trying vainly to do the strap up under his chin. It rather reminded me of that very first occasion when we heard gunfire at night – that was when Edmonton got it. I slipped a dress over my nightclothes, took Ruth downstairs, but had to wait ages for you to come down & unlock the back door so that we could go into the shelter. – The reason? you couldn't fasten your suspenders properly – did you stop to put your tie on too, or couldn't you find one to match your shirt? I can't quite remember.

There was also continual fretting as there could be as long as month between letters, and it took until 11 March 1943 for Sylvia to learn that her Christmas present to David had actually arrived. Other times a much-anticipated letter had, 'horror of horrors', been damaged in transit, with a precious photograph of David left scorched and the pages charred. Other letters, such as the airgraphs, (05.01.43), were:

so terrible short – you even left off the usual xx for Ruth & myself – but I shouldn't think that was through lack of time as much as that you forgot

She worried that he made no reference to the cash, gift and some photos she sent him. Then again (07.01.44):

I had been hoping for further news from you – but I suppose I ought to be thankful for the one a week I have been getting recently. I wonder if you are now receiving more of my back letters? I write three times, & sometimes four, every week, so that you should be getting news frequently.

Sylvia was also concerned about David's weight, down from his pre-war 13 stone, which she admits left him looking 'quite tubby', to 10 stone 6½lb. She comments: 'I find it difficult to visualise what you must look like' (24.01.43).

Sylvia refers to strains between Ruth and the two boys, Tony and Jeffrey, but David picks her up on what he reads as 'sarcasm' about Sam, her brother-in-law, in whose house she was living. Sylvia was initially defensive (02.03.43), 'I don't think I was', before acknowledging that:

perhaps these days I am inclined to be sarcastic unknowingly ... I hear so much about how much they are doing & what a strain things have been, that it tends to make my blood boil – sorry!

She adds that Sam was working from seven in the morning until six at night 'putting carbon paper in duplicate books', even when he knew the struggle Fay was having to keep the business going 'with the added trials of rationing'.

The situation deteriorated when the youngsters went down with measles (14.03.43). First to succumb was Tony:

We brought Tony's cot down into the dining room … The first few days
the room had to be in almost total darkness, & perhaps you can imagine
the strain.

Then Jeffrey was ill, followed a few days later by Ruth:

She wouldn't let me move an inch without her – I had to carry her around
& she was repeatedly sick at night. – One night we were both up every ten
minutes during her frequent coughing spells.

Sylvia ruefully concludes, 'See what you are missing Davie?' Given all this
it is not surprising that where once she had never had problems sleeping
at night, 'no matter how worried or upset I might be', now 'I simply
cannot fall asleep. I lie awake for ages, thinking about anyone & everyone
– mainly you' (09.01.43).

Once Sylvia started receiving letters again her mood lifted as well; at
one point she received three letter-cards on one day, then two more the
next morning: 'it's grand getting frequent news from you again.' It was
the quality, not just the quantity, as they were now 'far more interesting.
Your earlier ones have been all too short' (02.03.43). There was a sense
of a conversation between them, and her changing as a result, as in the
example above with her irritation with Sam. She was moved (04.03.43)
when she found out that David planned to:

send us money, – for Ruth's birthday & an anniversary gift, well, I felt like
weeping. I do appreciate your thoughtfulness so much. – It seems the army
has done that for you, if little else.

She was also (06.03.43) 'greatly cheered by your optimistic attitude
regarding the early end of the war.'

Something important shifts in her mood when she describes (19.03.43)
taking Ruth to see *Desert Victory*, which starred:

our husbands, our sons, & our sweethearts. Do you know, I felt so proud
of you for having taken part in that victory – proud of the hardships you
underwent, – proud of the pain of parting that I too have had to bear. –

I reproach myself any miserable note I may have allowed to creep into my letters, any depression I may have conveyed to you. It was so foolish of me – it should be so easy, here at home with normal comforts, to keep a smiling face & chins up. Perhaps it's because I love you too much that I feel your hardships so greatly. – God bless you darling, & keep you safe.

During the film, I asked Ruth to see if she could find you, but I'm afraid we didn't recognise you. Ruth excused herself with 'There were such a lot of soldiers, I couldn't find Daddy.' – The exercise we were shown the men under going was really strenuous. (Now I can realise how you lost those couple of stone.) And the men's bodies were tanned absolutely black – but you said you were very burnt too, didn't you?

Sylvia gained another perspective (25.03.43) from the radio reports of the journalist Godfrey Talbot. Based with the Eighth Army, he explained the importance of the mail and photos for the soldiers, where 'each letter is read & then re-read until the owner must know its contents almost by heart'. Talbot provided:

so many interesting talks about the life & activities of the desert soldier, that at times I can feel that I am really with you out there. I very often wish I were, in spite of the hardships & dangers.

• David: 'A Grand Day For Mail' •

In response to Sylvia's stories of her difficult times David advises (30.01.43) that she should:

Keep smiling, & don't forget that if you occasionally write moody letters, I understand & there is no need for appologies.

He notes (23.02.43) 'the sadness that creeps into your letters these days' and tries to reassure Sylvia that, while he has missed out on so much of Ruth's childhood, the same will not be true of the next one. For his own part he is:

still feeling fine, get a fit of moodiness now & again, passes of quickly, but the thought of you & baby are always with me.

He deeply regrets (26.02.43) the nine months since they were last together, but:

considering that we have many years ahead of us (P.G.) a meer year or year & half doesn't sound a lot (it's nice to kid ones self)

He continued to value the letters for their contact with home. He celebrated (in a letter dated November 1943, but from the context is almost certainly 31 March, Ruth's birthday) 'a grand day for mail' which included, from Sylvia, snaps of Sandown, a reminder 'of those good happy days', and papers, 'the 'D.W.' [the communist *Daily Worker*] two issues of Reynolds [a Sunday socialist paper], also Lou's little parcel of books ... you can imagin how pleased I was with all of you. "Bless 'em all."' This was, as he put at the top of the page, 'baby's birthday Bless her', and he hoped that Sylvia had bought her something nice from him. Also, their wedding anniversary, 8 April, was also near.

Regarding the family, he worried about Lionel, 'that crazy kid', who had become involved with a girl in Canada, and he wondered if his brother, Alf, would follow suit and bring home a French girl. He muses that it is 'lucky that I'm married, other-wise I think I would go native'. He describes losing his watch and wallet, including his honeymoon snaps, all because 'we were being unpleasantly shelled, so we had to retire in the hurry of it'. This was regrettable but 'dear, remember they can be replaced'.

On another occasion (11.02.43) family fortunes led him to muse about his army career, or lack of it. One brother-in-law, Ralph, was about to be promoted; Lionel was a flying officer; 'a remote relation' through Sam was a major; and one or two friends were army MOs: 'We are certainly in society.' That he remained a gunner should not have worried Sylvia since 'I always liked being in the rank & file, & sweetheart it's the way I want it, & being temprementilly lazy it just suits me'.

• Sylvia and David: The Strains of Sexual Feelings and Sustaining a Relationship •

One issue that emerged was the lack of physical closeness that was clearly a vital aspect of their married life.[1] This was difficult to address in a letter, though Sylvia had already commented that 'it is rather awkward being intimate with a piece of paper', but nonetheless went on in the same letter (18.08.42) to describe how she had been accosted in the street one evening and had warned David, after hearing that he was off to Cairo on leave, not to bring home an illegitimate child. David adds to this (11.02.43) when he writes:

> remember this dear, with my little family I want no substitutions or more important still any additions, as I don't want to come home under those circumstances.

The sexual temptations were everywhere it seemed. Sylvia describes Betty, not yet 20, working as 'a dance hostess' and having 'a thoroughly good time', becoming 'very thick with the American soldiers'. Then Lionel, training with the RAF in Canada, scandalised the family by announcing that he was getting married. This was without having 'broached the subject' with Millie, his mother and the formidable eldest daughter of the family. Not to mention, the girl was 'a redhead' who he had known for less than seven weeks. A redeeming feature was that she was at least Jewish (10.03.43).

The subject arose for David and Sylvia when David described (15.01.43) going to a 'real good' concert where there had been:

> two nice, pretty girls … The sight of them was too much for us, we are still walking about in a semi-dazzed condition.

Sylvia (09.01.43) had seen a film of an Ensa concert held in the desert, also with two girls in the troop, 'one dark & the other fair'. She noticed the effect on the men, who 'from one or two close-ups of the audience … seemed to be thoroughly enjoying it'. Sylvia writes that David's reactions had 'amused' her. 'I suppose it does make a break for you though, however poor the show might be.'

Then Sylvia gives news of the wife of a good friend of David's who was also now fighting away from home. Her behaviour had already given rise to a 'certain amount of gossip' but she then, it seems, deserted her home and young child. Sylvia writes:

> I wondered, somehow, if it were right to condemn [her] entirely – it is her nature. I thought maybe I would be more content if I followed her example – but I haven't the guts, as I suppose you know.

David's response (24.01.43) was to 'risk the censor' by becoming 'very sentimental' in his reflections on the life they once shared:

> It seems such a long time since I've seen you & enjoyed my full rights as a married man, & believe me dear, that though I am normally sexed, I am beginning to miss you very much.

> The photograph of you with baby & Mother, tells me what I am missing, you really look beautiful & more seductive than ever, as a matter of fact you seem to have got a little fuller in the figure & face, & it certainly adds to your charms, it is very reminiscent of the girl I took to be my bride.

> It is a ritual with me, these days to look at that photograph every day, then to look at you, & to regretfully ponder over the beauty, charm & the delights of sex that is so far away.

> It will soon be six years that we now have been married, & it is with great happiness that I look back on that certain day April 8th 1937 when I took unto my-self a wife. I have no regrets but a great deal of thanks, that I should have found favour in your eyes.

> Since that day, which was only a happiness of excitement, uncertainty, it developed through those six years into a happiness of knowledge & fulfilment. The knowledge that if marriage be a lottery, I won the greatest of all prizes, a perfect wife.

Fulfilment being, that you have fulfilled all my intellectual & physical wants. In both those things I was indeed rich, then came baby, & you could not have found a happier man.

In looking back-ward, those early days with baby was great fun. Remember that Sunday when I took baby round to the butchers to get some meat? I was supposed to take her for a walk after I got the meat but I was only gone about five minutes. You chided me with that I was ashamed to walk with the pram, my excuse being that I thought it was going to rain. Then again those blitz's days, our nights to-gether in the Anderson shelter on the hammock with baby in the corner in her portable basket, the songs we sang & rhymes we made up.

It was only possible to do those things in trying times, if you are really happy. Not only that, but my admiration & adoration for you increased tremendously, when I was called up & you took over the shop. You managed it well − bravely stood up to all that Jerry dished out nearly every night. Looking back, I must have been a really selfish chap to subordinate every thing else to keeping the shop going. There was you & a young baby not only keeping the shop going, but being subjected to heavy night bombing, you did not grumble but kept that delightful chin of yours well up. Our sexual life was completely harmonious, I only hope that in bed I gave you as much pleasure as you gave me.

Sylvia (12.03.43) was 'very thrilled' by these words:

Do you know, I have read, & also re-read, that letter at least three times − you must indeed have been in a sentimental mood to have written in such a strain. You give a picture of myself that makes me think I must be something of a heroine − I almost admire myself. Yet they were happy days, even the trying blitz nights in the Anderson, just we two & baby at first.

Glancing through that letter yet again, I feel most deeply how you must have felt to have let yourself go in this way. − But you old so & so, you knew I would enjoy reading it, didn't you? I only wish I could reply in the same strain, but you know how easily I blush. I think, darling, our pleasures were mutual – I'm sure I can give claim to as great a part as you.'[2]

Later (08.04.43) Sylvia names what else she misses in David: 'your companionship, having someone to turn to – to ask questions of, to explain things I don't understand, & to discuss things with.' She links this to how often 'I think of what you must be enduring while I am tucked away comfortably in bed. – And Davie, I never cease praying for your safety.'

• 'The Best News of all': The Mareth Line, Wadi Akarit and the Fall of Sousse •

David and Sylvia were sharply taken away from these reflections: the new tropical kit he had been issued may have made him 'really look smart', but it had another purpose. He was to be thrust back into the fighting, and the next stage of the fight in North Africa was the Mareth Line.[3]

David describes the battle as follows (04.04.43):

> The best news of all you must know by now we have smashed the Mereth line & got Rommel again on the run, this time he can't run far, & as far as the Eighth Army is concerned the North Africa affair is over, it is a real relief. To make you more proud of your fighting husband, it might interest you know that I was one of the lads to help & smash it, it was a bitter do, but I came through OK, we are resting now, & leaving it to others to chase him.

He goes on to say that:

> I was no behind line merchant, in the thick of things the whole way through, am rather surprised of myself, for being able to stand up to things in general, I did not think I had it in me.

Following the fall of Sousse (12.04.43), his new position was some 10 miles north of Gabes, which allowed him to 'do quite a bit of bathing in the Gulf'.

It was a few weeks later (23.04.43) that he returned to the details of the fighting. He describes how, after pushing forward to take up battle positions and five days of patrols reconnoitring the enemy lines, at 4 a.m. on 6 April, in complete darkness, and following a fifteen-minute barrage, a general attack was launched:

> Well dearest one … I was in the thick of things when we broke Jerry at the 'Wadi Akarit' I think history will record that a greater battle than the Mareth doo, & more far reaching, because after that it was flat country and Sousse had to fall.

> After Sousse some 30 miles north come the natural defences of ranges of hills in depth going to-wards Tunis, it was the battle for these hills I was next in action for, well again it meant sleepless nights firing and digging, we took the first hills, & I went beyond Enfindaville (look at the map). Then luck would have it, we were withdrawn, and I am back about 100 miles, not far from Sfax. I think it was because our Div. was really battle weary, & we had to go back for a rest.

> It was an interesting journey going back, when going up to battle all our travelling is done in the night, but this time it was day light, we went through Sousse & a lot of fair sized villages, & there was quite a lot of French people there, they all gave us the V sign, but strangely enough it was without enthusiasm or smiles. I suppose they gave the Natzi salute with the same indifference.

> Poor people, the war in any case only brought them broken homes, and hungry mouths, only the natives seemed made up with us.

> Incidently on the way back our barter system worked fine, we got three loaves of bread & 53 eggs. I bet you could have done with them.

This meant that:

> the war is over out here, please don't ask me 'little man what now' my guess is as good as yours, so please don't worry about it, things are cushy now, so why worry.

The news was being closely followed at home (10.04.43):

> While I was reading the African news this morning Ruth, pointing to the map of Tunisia asked 'Where's Daddy now?' – I estimated a spot a little north of Gabes, & showed her the place on the map. – 'And where's Ronald?' she queried. – I pointed out a spot quite nearby, at which she got very excited 'Oh goodie – Daddy's nearly caught Ronald'.

Then, in a letter on David's birthday (12.04.43), Sylvia describes switching on the six o'clock news and hearing:

> the grand tidings that Sousse has fallen. This is really splendid news – good work, David, & keep it up! Mother is almost as excited about it as Ruth & I are. Ruth is jumping around singing 'Good old Daddy' – she naturally presumes that all the successes from N. Africa are accomplished by you alone – what hero worship!

• *'Dear Familiar Things': A Time to Reflect on Religion, Politics, Food and the Meaning of Home, May 1943* •

After this adrenalin rush of battle the letters shift in mood. David (01.05.43) repeats a joke he has heard:

> A child of three once asked her mother in referring to her father who was in the army 'who is that man that comes dashing in & out & seems to know us?'

With Passover approaching, David imagines (12.04.43) that back home 'every body is very busy with Pesach preparations', and he hopes they are 'managing O.K. as far as Kosher food is concerned'. He knows he will 'miss the Matzos & the wine, especially the cakes, most of all I'll miss you'. He then reflects (19.04.05) how:

> if old Rommel would have cleared off I might have been spending it in Tunis, or better still if it would not have been for Hitler, I would have

been with you my darling wife & my three year old daughter (Bless them) celebrating it in the good old fasioned way at your father's place.

I shall certainly be asking the 'Kashers' to-night & with feeling say 'Oh God why is this night different from any other'. The answer lays I suppose with the 'Guilty Men', but Please God next year I hope to say those words with joyfulness & gladness, for I shall be holding your & Ruthies hands at the table.

Do you know Sylvia that I have become quite religious in my thoughts, comforts civilisation & peace, gives you strength in yourself, & you become egoistical inclined. But Danger & destruction makes you realise how helpless you are, then your thoughts turn to something that is greater than your-self, & that is God.

So sweetheart mine, do not be surprised, if I tell you that I say my prayers every night, strange things happen & they give you a new start in life. Glad you like the way <u>we</u> boys are cleaning up Jerry, the papers are giving us all the headlines, well if it makes you folks in Blighty feel good, we have done our Job.[4]

On 23 April he actually spends:

Sida night … firing a barrage till early hours of the morning, a tiring & strange Sida night, I hope I never experience another like it.

Sylvia's response (03.05.43) is that:

It's funny you saying that you have become religious lately; I so often feel tempted otherwise. True, I still derive a great deal of consolation from praying – it seems to be the only thing one can fall back on, but that isn't religion is it? I somehow didn't have any patience this year for Pesach – it all seemed such a farce. Yet something made me insist on changing over the crocks etc. – Fay didn't want to bother. So many things we couldn't help eat that week I wouldn't have dreamed of doing normally. Yet it didn't worry me as much as I thought it would – Anyway, I'm more pleased that you

should seek comfort by praying. There are so many prayers being said for
you, day & night. – God bless you always.

However, her feelings are contradictory. Earlier (29.04.43) she had written:

Pesach is over, & we have just cleared away & brought out all the old china
etc. I do so hope that I'll be doing this job for myself next year P.G. in our
own home once again. Is it possible do you think? I hope & pray that it
may be so every minute of the day.

Then (15.05.43) she regrets that there was 'no real Pesach this year ... The
usual special items were right off the menu'.

Her main attention stays with the war, forgiving David the lack of
letters: 'in view of the renewed activities, I don't suppose you have very
much time for writing' (29.04.43). She keeps David up to date on bits and
pieces of domestic news, visits from family, sister Millie with Mick and the
twins, an unexpected letter from Alf, Lionel's forthcoming marriage, and
how this 'starts off the next generation,– though we hadn't really finished
with the previous one', and stories of Ruth and how she now knew that
'a "genkleman"' is one who is 'walking by the curb – lady's on other side'.
Then (02.05.43) she comments on Fay 'having a doze on the armchair'
and 'the row going on ... It's surprising what a noise Jeff & Tony do make,
& Ruth certainly contributes more than her fair share'.

David referred to a film they had both seen, *They all Kissed the Bride*.
Sylvia remembered (29.06.43) the phrase 'we shall both cross the great
divide together' (Sylvia's emphasis) from this, and she comments that this
'is a hope I earnestly repeat'. Indeed:

That opportunity almost presented itself on a certain April evening a
couple of years ago – but it seems that the fates had decided otherwise. It
might have saved a lot of heartache now – I pray that our future happiness
will compensate us for trying days.

Recent alerts in London showed that this danger was a continuing one,
and Sylvia (29.06.43) had to assure David that:

We are O.K. here, so don't get worried about us. You are in the front line of battle & must be very used to what we are occasionally given a taster of. It has now been said with some authority, that blitzes such as we have known them will not again occur in this country. Of course, these tip & run raids also do enough damage, & the solitary planes that creep through to the London area cause some disturbance too, but we are keeping our end up.

More routine details of daily life are regularly referred to (03.05.43). David urges Sylvia to spend some money he has sent home, but she admits:

Afraid I haven't yet broken into your £5. As far as the bike is concerned – well, Marie [a sister-in-law] has a decent one of Edward's, & I asked her if she'd care to sell it as I know she wants to buy him a bigger one. But she said I needn't worry about <u>buying</u> it from her – as soon as they are able to obtain one for Edward, Ruth will most certainly <u>have</u> his red one. After having asked her, I don't like to get one elsewhere (even supposing it is possible to do so.) But she has been trying for ages to get one, so perhaps I will put an advert in the Ilford Recorder, & see what comes of it.

You suggest that I buy some new clothes with my share of the cash. What makes you think I need any? – or is it just that a woman always feels she needs new clothes? – Maybe, but not in wartime – anyway, have you forgotten the clothes rationing scheme? (But don't worry about us – Ruth & I manage famously on our coupons.) Anyway, darling, I don't really have the necessity for wearing a great variety of clothes. I did buy a new dress shortly before Xmas, & Fay & I both bought coats early this year, so, with the usual minor additions as times go by, I shall manage fine.

But I shall break into the money this weekend at last. I have fixed an appointment for a perm – Betty had hers done a couple of months ago, & it saves such a lot of bother with the curlers every night, that I felt tempted. (I only wish I'd thought of it while you were here – look at all the time I'd have saved – I'm sure we could have put it to good use.)

Food also featured (25.05.43):

Ruth had her first tomato of the season yesterday. Mother had a few over
the weekend & saved one for Ruth's tea. She was most excited, & when I
said it was an 'orange', she agreed 'Yes, it's an orange.' – That's how much
she knows of both these items. I looked longingly at the tomato, & asked
if I might have a piece. She quite willingly gave me a quarter, & when she
had finished hers & was eating the rest of her salad, I asked 'Would you like
this piece too?' – Before I could say another word she picked it up saying
'All right – I'll have it if you don't want it.' – She certainly hadn't needed
much persuading.

This contrasts rather with David's account (14.05.43) of how he was
'eating plenty of good food, oranges, bananas & ices, & seeing I've got
something like £20 on me, I won't go short of anything'.

The first day of May, the traditional day to celebrate the socialist and
Labour movement, prompts the observation (02.05.4?):

If you were home you may have been tempted to join in the demonstration
– instead of which you are marching many hundreds of miles away from the
old route. Makes me wonder which march is of greater help to the 'Cause.'
I suppose today, in Trafalgar Square, there will be the usual speeches, the
usual agitation for a second front by people who won't be called upon to
take part in it. It really is remarkable how enthusiastic an unaffected person
can be. Even in the early days when Rommel was steadily moving towards
Alexandria & it seemed as if nothing could stop the Africa Corps, over
here they were still clamouring for a second front. Of course, it must come,
but surely in its own good time. Your D.W. annoys me sometimes. They
always have a grievance over something. I'm always interested to see what
complaint they can make over the handling of any particular affair. – Still,
in the long run, I suppose their fight is our fight & that is the main thing.

On another level Sylvia was busying herself with the outstanding business
of the earlier war damage, which raised both practical and emotional
concerns (13.05.43):

I shall be going over to Walthamstow next Thursday, to get our war
damage claim assessed. Miriam is coming up from Aylesbury for the day,

& I shall meet her at the store-house so that our goods can be separated. The District Valuer had written to me again, & asked me to [missing words due to censorship of the other page] the furniture separated [missing] my claim [missing] And, as I think I told you last time I wanted this job done, the local Council couldn't touch the goods unless Miriam & I were both present. Anyway, the Valuer will join us there too, & the salvaged items can be assessed. I'm rather dreading seeing it all again – it has been lying in that place for over two years now, neglected, uncared for. When Annie [a sister] had the rest of her home brought from Queen Elizabeth Walk, she said she found the carpet & rugs moth-eaten, & everything greatly deteriorated. Still, it's no use getting upset over it – it just can't be helped – I can't take the things out of store – I've nowhere to put them, so they'll just have to stay put until after the War. Then, please God, there will be a new home for three, & what has been lost will be replaced (in more respects than one).

Sylvia subsequently (20.05.43) returns to the story:

I saw all those dear familiar things; I found in a drawer that old blue lumber cardigan you used to wear in the shop; odd scraps of paper with shop takings entered on them; that photo Bob took of us with baby when she was only nine weeks old (this was badly torn in the corner, but is precious to me – I've brought it home). I can't give details in this short space as to how the claim worked out, so shall write of it again next time. – The total, however was a few pounds of what I claimed – £259 – furniture, shop fittings, personal clothing etc.

This provokes a series of thoughts and hopes:

You say also, that once this war is over we will live again – no more stinting & saving, we shall get out of life what it owes us. That is just how I feel about it – all that struggle to make a home & a decent enough business, putting back every penny that we could into the shop & where did it get us? Jerry simply blasted the lot in one blitz, & what were we left with? Our lives – (& everyone kept impressing how important that was. – True, how would the 8th Army ever have made that thrust from Alamein without you?) – Part of our home that was salvaged, &, thank God, enough capital to begin all over again & also the will to do so. I wonder if you realise how anxious I am to make another start, somewhere, anywhere, just the three of us again.

The pleasure of getting the claim met was then thwarted (9.06.43) by further complications:

I don't recall whether I have told you that I must remove our furniture from the Council's store. It is a Government order that these storehouses must be cleared as soon as possible. I have been along to the Citizen's Advice Bureau, but it seems nothing can be done. They suggested that I re-store privately, & then apply to the War Service Grants for financial help to meet the expense. But to say 're-store', is easier said than done – all the storage firms I have tried haven't an inch to spare, & I must get the stuff removed by June 30th. Stemmings – do you remember them? – seem to think they'll have space in about three or four weeks, so I daresay W'stow will oblige until then – they'll have to. They roughly estimate the charge as being 35/- – £2 per month – that's without seeing how much, (or how little) there is. They can't say really until the goods are stacked & how much space they occupy. I have already written to the Service Grants, but if they don't help, well it will have to cost £25 per year. I only hope it won't be for too many years, that's all.

Later (06.07.43) Sylvia returned to the council store 'to separate a few more items that were still mixed up with Miriam's', then to find somewhere to restore the furniture:

but I've had such a job finding someone with even an inch of space free. I went to W'stow Town Hall last Tuesday, & saw the housing manager. He was very considerate, & suggested that the housing dept. should find me a flat. I explained that I wasn't able to set up home again during the war, so he suggested several local firms which may have storage space. Only one of the five or six he mentioned was able to take on my job. The only annoying part was that they insisted on doing the removal as well – at a charge of £3. W'stow Council were prepared to do it for me – free. I have been quoted 7/6 per week, & am also insuring against fire – a further 25/- per year. – And so, David, we are moving tomorrow morning – at 90/c.

To make matters worse she then met and joined up with a couple who were seeking accommodation. They visited a flat, which, since they liked it, was immediately offered to them. Sylvia envies the friend:

> being able to shift her furniture into a home, & not into another store house. But then she has, a husband with her, & there is no reason why she shouldn't have her own home again.

The emotions for both David and Sylvia were running high since this coincided with the first anniversary of their parting and both comment on how this left them feeling. For Sylvia (25.05.43):

> They say that the first ten years are the worst. I reminded Ruth today that it is now a whole year since we last saw you for a couple of hours, but I'm afraid she didn't really appreciate how very long a time a year is. Long that is, when it is spent apart – time seemed to fly when we were together – especially those short seven day leave. – I'd more than welcome one now though. I wish I knew how long the parting will have to be – or perhaps it is better that I don't know. – Well that is enough sentiment for the moment.

For David (26.05.43) it had:

> been a year of mixed emotions, of pride & of sorrow … This parting from you has moved me a great deal, believe me dear, life can be very empty, & my emptiness started the day I left you standing at the corner of the Green Man.

> That picture of you, will never fade from my mind as long as I live & P.G. I hope that to be a long time.

> I thank God who gave us intellect gave us also the ability to adapt oneself to any circumstances, that is the way of life.

> Soon I hope the people of the world will be dictating a policy of the 'pursuit of happiness' and then dearest you & baby will be found amongst them, until then it just got to be chins up all the time.

I appreciate your remarks re. the 'DW' & also the Second Front. It will come all in good time, & that must be decided by those who know best.

Well love I am still OK & feeling fine, no worries except that I want to get back to you quickly, & that's the kind of complaint everybody has got out here.

Love & regards to all at Woodford.

My bestest love to you & Ruth.

Yours ever,

David

• *Tunis and Bizerta: 'Seems Like Walking on Air'* •

Returning to the war (11.05.43), David reports how Tunis and Bizerta had made everyone 'seem like walking on air ... it's one phase of the war ended'.[5] He follows this (13.05.10) with the prediction that 'Italy looks like giving up already, a few more heavy raids & her mind will be made up', which indicated that 'Germany must be very jitterey'. He anticipated a landing in Europe, which would mean that:

> the peoples in all the occupied countries will be with us, & Germany will not be able to fight both, that is a strong army on it's front & a army of sabaters at its rear.

This rush of enthusiasm, where he was happy with the 'sacrifices I had to make for freedom & democracy & a Churchill cigar' (11.05.43), is followed (23.05.43) by complaints about how army life consists of:

> the routine, discipline and barrack behaviour ... once again the hours for washing & shaving, is being regulated, also the way to act when we go out, yes my dear it appears that only in the army, you wash every day

& your appearance looked after. It's a wonder you don't have to tie your handkerchief to your lapel, just like you did when you went to school.

One break in the routine came with leave in Alexandria; his letter (17.05.43) is given in full:

I AM WRITING THIS FROM ONE OF THE CENTRES OF THE
UNION DEFENCE FORCE INSTITUTES.
  (Y.M.C.A – TOC H)
  MIDDLE EAST

My dearest Sylvia,

Still enjoying myself, but this is my last day. I'm not sorry it is finishing, its made a darn good brake but I miss you & baby too much to really enjoy myself, its been a pleasant form of escapism & as such a good time was had by all.

Alex is a very expensive place, bags of good food, for example for dinner we might have, chicken soup, roast chicken, chips & veg, followed by strawberrys & cream coffee & pastries, costing about 30 piastres (a piastre is worth 2½ d) that is what we spend every time.

I have not yet ridden in a car (tram I mean) the taxi & horse carriage being only good enough for us, our favourite drink for the evening is spirits which is a lot cheeper than beer.

Went to the races on Saturday & was quite excited & thrilled, lost about 40 piastres, I only backed two runners, still it was fun, flicks every night, but it has been a poor week as far as films have been concerned, the only decent film being, 'The pied piper' do you know of it.

I have found that I have not spent all my money, so I went shopping for you & baby, three pairs of silk stockings for you. I hope you will like them, for baby a hand bag & four hankies. I am now praying that they shall reach you safe & in good condition, shall be upset if they don't.

I have taken a lot of photos & am going to carry out my usual procedure that is to send them on one at a time. I hope you will like the one enclosed, it's a bit dark, but clear enough.

I'm looking forward to getting back to my unit, & its for only one reason that is mail. I miss your letters, & I am sure there is quite a few waiting for me. (Bless you).

Now that Hitler is definitely on the defensive, & on the <u>losing side</u> I'm hoping for a speeding finish to all this horror & darkness that is around us all, & that I will soon be in the light & beauty of your pleasant company. God Bless you & Ruth.

My love to all at Woodford

X for you   Yours Ever
X for Ruth   David

Back at base (24.06.43) he passed his time by learning to drive and playing cricket, and he describes how he is 'sitting now in the canteen writing this, the wireless is playing, the sun is shining, the weather is hot'. Then he turns to Sylvia's letter-card in which she spoke of their parting a year ago:

Well do I remember it, it was a crisis in our emotions, we smiled, but how near to tears we were, it is now all forgotten, I am just an imaginary David & you an imaginary Sylvia, only real in our dreams, (& is Ruth real or just a figment in my imagination?)

Did I once live as a human being, sit in a chair & eat at a table? Did I once enjoy the love of a beautiful woman, & enjoy the beauty of living?

Yes –Yes, I think I did, what brings the past back to me? your letters sweetheart mine, I know dear, that in the near future I shall grasp again the joy of living, that is why I thank God for the women he gavest me & for the child you brought me, for that reason I laugh & dream, dreams that will come true.

He goes on to say:

> Now dear let me get something off my chest, & please Sylvia take this in the spirit that we are just talking to ourselves, & perhaps talking foolishly, but we used to talk like this in bed, & like all talks it used to lead from the birth to the grave.

> Well it is this, while I was in action, & people were dying, I did not want to write about if I should die, but now death is far away, I feel I can write now — If I should not come back (God forbid) I want you to marry again, I don't want a beautiful womanhood to develop into a sour widowhood, nor do I think you should live alone, I would not want you to live in the past of a dead love, the future belongs to the living 'let the dead bury the dead.' ... A woman must love somebody, if she has no man, but has a child, she by her emotional love for her daughter, she will sap her independence, cramp her style, & even interfere because of jealousy with her love affairs, this I do not want to happen to Ruth, so you see my point, don't let it worry you, <u>I am coming home</u> & I am glad I've got it off my chest.

This provokes a strong response in Sylvia (04.07.43). She was already vulnerable after a visit to relatives in which she was left with the older generation, her contemporaries having gone out for the day. Sylvia ironically comments:

> the weather was grand & I couldn't expect it of them to waste a day entertaining visitors ... you weren't there, & somehow without you I am no one – I just drift into obscurity.

So she made a plea to David:

> don't write me another letter like the one I received on Friday. I'm scared even to consider the thought that you may not come back to me. To feel for the rest of my life as I have felt for the past year – to spend my leisure hours as I have had to spend them since you've been gone. Sorry, David, that I'm writing this way – I hadn't intended to, but it must be the mood I'm in. When I received your green envelope on Friday, I read your letter

& considered the contents quite seriously – in the same [illegible] as I dare say you wrote it.

You take a most unselfish attitude regards the future – I suppose it is the sanest way. I wonder if I would say the same thing to you if the position were reversed …

But David, do you really think that I could find another mug? Another person who would put up with me & my nonsense the way you always have? And, of course, is there another human being I could tolerate for more than five minutes after having been so thoroughly spoilt by you? So you see, my darling, its simply no use trying to palm me off, & you'll just have to come back, safe & sound – and soon!! (By the way, suppose I had already spent Ruth's £500 by the time I re-married, what would I do then? – But joking aside, that is a point to consider. But knowing your wishes, I'd see that amount was always untouched – just in case. – Bless you David, for thinking of her future too.)

• *The Invasion of Italy, 'The Fear of Death is Always at Hand'* •

For all of David's determination about 'coming home', there were to be many delays. Sylvia carefully followed the news of the war; below is one typical example (05.06.43):

> News does continue to be good as far as we at home are concerned – the unity at last of the two French Generals is a great relief. Also the success as yet of the revolution in the Argentine is heartening. – News now that Churchill is back in England forecasts, perhaps, some new step in the progress of the war. Well, the sooner this whole affair is finished the better I for one, shall like it.

She was also excited (15.07.43) by the return of Japanese prisoners of war. The press stories include a photo which could be that of an old friend of Ralph's who had been missing in action, presumed killed. Then came (25.07.43) the radio announcement of Mussolini's resignation:

Oh, David, what far reaching effects this may have – it surely must shorten the War. This news will surely be history by the time this letter reaches you, so I had better make no further comments. I should hate to feel how wrong I was.

Sylvia wanting to know (05.06.43) 'exactly where you are' prompted David's reply (21.06.43): 'please don't ask me what I'm doing, or where I am, & censorship is really hot, leading articles in the papers can tell you more than I can.'

He does (01.05.43), nevertheless, refer to Tripoli. He:

did not enjoy it much, it was a very hungry city & in concequence we could not get much to eat, still it was nice to at least say you had been there.

He also refers to the 'Lybian sun', adding:

I know all this sound rather mysterious, but perhaps in a week or two I may be able to tell you where I am.

However, he was prepared to say that his location was:

beautiful, its very hot, that is to expected, the evening grand, grapes, oranges, lemons, pears, tomatoes, grow all around us, not forgetting walnuts & almonds, I should come again a nice place to tour.

It's a pity I was just becoming conversant with Arabic, & now I've got to learn different tongue, still I hope I'm not in this country that long.

David was actually a part of Montgomery's preparation for the move into Europe, Operation Husky, the storming of the beaches of Avolo on 10 July. David hoped (01.08.43) that by the time Sylvia received his letter 'the island will be ours and Italy also might be out of it', thus seriously shortening the war. This might be a sign of the soldiers' collective eternal optimism and/or a determined effort to cheer Sylvia up, for he starts by chiding her 'Don't be so pessimistic, all this stuff about no use saying "be home soon"'.

Sylvia again followed the progress of the war in the papers (10.07.43):

So at last the invasion of Sicily has begun – it seems to herald the final phase of the war. We have been warned of a long & hard struggle still ahead, but being on the offensive & having such great confidence in the victorious outcome, one cannot but help feeling optimistic as to an early finish. My thoughts & prayers are ever with you; good luck darling, & may God be with you during these coming days of trial & hardship.

David enjoyed his new base, moved by the beauty of Sicily, where (12.08.43):

some parts here really takes your breath away. Mt. Etna dominates the whole view round here, its like an immense shadow against a blue background, with white smoke continuously coming from it. It was something like this that made Keats write 'a thing of beauty is a joy for ever'.

He also picked up (10.08.43) 'a smattering' of Italian, which allowed him to get:

quite chatty with the civvies, they seem to welcome us with open arms, hope after the war we can give something better than the conditions they are living under now.

In the same letter, David makes some further observations:

Women grow old quite quickly, you can't wonder at it, they marry at 14–15 years, at 20 they have two or three bambinos, they work hard, & live terrible, no sanitary conditions in existence, cooking is done by a wood fire in the open air, water is drawn from a well, they are all very poorly dressed, & not too clean at that.

Subsequently (01.09.43) he revises his opinion:

A word about their women, though poor, they dress well, make a great fuss over their hair, which is always neatly arranged, dark & quite good looking,

& like in Egypt & North Africa, they ooze femininity, daring to show all
their curves, & as they say in the classics, they have plenty, it makes me really
home sick, & me being a very moral man am the wolf in the fabel & say
sour grapes.

Elsewhere (06.08.43) David reflects further on the action he was involved
in and the degree to which the Allied advance, once the initial invasion
was achieved, then slowed down:[6]

Now that it is nearly over I don't think the censor ought to object to these
remarks, for I will try & give you what 50 Div. did in Sicily, so you can at
least know in what part of Sicily I was in.

I will leave out for the time being my fears & reactions, when we were told
we were going to invade Sicily, every thing seemed to have been planned
perfectly, even to the smallest detail, we were even given a 'Soldiers guide
to Sicily'.

After about a week afloat, the day came, the first lot went towards land at
1.30am, it was dark & a deathly stillness hang listlessly in the night air. I felt
really sorry for the infantry, it must have been a hell of a rotten job, but his
job is a rotten one at the best of times.

I was leaning over the side watching the land, nothing could be heard, it
was very strange then, but light came, the Infantry had the positions well
in hand with hardly any opposition. & our Regt. landed in Avolan beaches
without any trouble, & four hours later Sircuss (not sure of this spelling)
was taken.

It was the next day that trouble started ME's kept coming over straffing
and bombing & it was certainly sticky & the road we were travelling was
certainly dangerous.

We raced on, by-passing Siracuos, going thru., Florida, Sortino, Corleotina
& Lentina, & the population gave us a real royal welcome, it was good to
see it, in the meantime we had hardly any sleep, & we were clearly tired, it

was Lentini, that we ourselves did a bit of mopping up, capturing about 11 light armoured cars, some motor bikes, & about 130 Italian prisoners, we laugh about it now, but we were a little scared then.

Well the next phase of the battle was a hold up, we were held up just south of Catania, & we could not shift him, but the Americans & Canadians were out flanking him & he had to move back & now we were going to chase him good & proper everything looks O.K. now.

David (06.08.43) then shifts to the important matter of marking Sylvia's birthday. He hopes she is 'celebrating it up West' or perhaps in Frome (the village in Somerset where family members had gone to escape London). He is sure of his intentions: he has two bottles of wine 'and my pals are going to toast the "Lady of the day Sylvia" isn't that nice & they all send their regards & best wishes'. He adds the postscript:

My bestest love to you & Ruth, God bless you both & my thoughts are more than ever with you on the day. Here is wishing that I wont be lonely for long P.G.

Your most loving husband

David

For Sylvia the passing time was almost unendurable. She writes how (22.07.43):

I thought somehow, that as time went by I would get used to the idea of you being away; yet, after more than a whole year, I think I feel our parting even more badly than I did when you first left. You once advised that I should forget about you – forget that I ever had a husband if only you could realise how impossible that is. – At times, when I don't hear from you for some while, you seem to become very vague – but Ruth's continuous references to you soon bring you back very vividly in my mind. Last night when I was putting her to bed she kissed your photo & said lovingly 'I do love my daddy.' – I then said 'How do you know? – You don't really know him.' She looked so crest fallen that I felt ashamed of myself – then she asked wistfully 'Is he nice.' –'Yes,' I told her, 'very nice.' – 'And do you love him very much?' she asked. 'Yes I love him very much' – 'Then,' she answered triumphantly, 'I love him 's well.'

It seemed kind of –'if I love you, I'll love your dog.' – But really David, the number of times that we mention your name during the course of each & every day is more than you would imagine. Your ears must be burning continuously. But honestly darling, my dearest wish is that she will love you even as much as I do – the real you, I mean, not the imaginary you that we talk about. – Please God when you come home you & our baby will have the rest of your lives to get to really & truly know each other.

The last letter I received from you, which was also the most recently written, dated June 27th, was the pencilled one you wrote during an odd moment or two. It was only a scribbled note really, & the one I received previous to that was your green envelope of June 24th. This was the letter in which you went into detail as to re-marriage etc. In view of the present renewed activity in Sicily, I have re-read that letter a few times & can see it in a calm, almost cold blooded light. Yet you say that 'now death is far away, I feel I can write' & that 'while I was in action & people were dying, I did not want to write about if I should die.' – That is of some consolation to me – to know that you felt that at that time death was far away. But at times like these the fear of death must always be at hand, & I pray to God every minute of the day & night that you may be spared to us. At times I feel very selfish to pray for so much when there are so many others suffering such great hardship. But if this is selfishness, then may it be my greatest failing.

Good luck my darling, & keep smiling – remember, chins up!

One of the ways she retained her memories and feeling of David was, as ever, through photos. She sent him pictures of the family and received his in return. She describes (08.08.43) how:

I think I've had all your photos now – five studio ones; two sitting by the steps; one having your shoes polished; one sitting in a carriage with your

pals; & of course, the banana eating one. – There is also one small snap
which you said was taken by a pal, & of which further copies should be
coming. On the whole I think they are very good – I, personally, like every
one, especially the small snap & also the serious studio one. You say you are
still the same old Davie – I won't believe that – a lot more impatient, well, I
won't mind that – & as to more character in your love making, well I don't
think I ever complained, but I won't mind that either.

• *September 1943, the Fifth Anniversary of the War:* *'And What Exactly are we Fighting For?'* •

Come September (04.09.43) and the fifth anniversary of the start of the
war, David writes:

> It seems now that nothing can stop the Allies, the speed of our gains will I
> think exceed that of the Germans in the first years of the war, the next six
> months should see first the collapse of Italy (which is at hand now) second
> the fall of the Balkans due to the gains of the Russians, thirdly the fight in
> Germany proper I'm confident that victory will come speedily, & quickly,
> & then let us hope it will have been really a war to end all wars.

Sylvia shares the upbeat mood and also reports on her stay with her family
in Frome (09.09.43). This was very enjoyable but she also describes a visit
to a fair:

> One evening when we went, a biggish crowd of coloured Americans had
> come into the town. Ruth was most interested, & drew my attention to
> several 'chocolate soldiers with chocolate faces' who were clowning on a
> roundabout. Her reference to them being 'chocolate' rather surprised me as
> she has never queried as to why her doll Topsy should be black when her
> other dolls are white.

> These soldiers are stationed several miles outside of the town, but I
> understand that there were several nearby here a few months back. There
> was a bit of trouble at one of the local dances though, so a colour bar

was imposed. Then the local inhabitants raised a shindy & it was thought advisable to shift the men further out of town. Betty tells me that the coloured American soldier is also not allowed at the Red+ Club to which she goes. It rather makes me wonder what exactly you are fighting for, & also what they are fighting for – there is talk of freedom & rights. I always feel so sorry when I see these fellows – they are called Americans, yet are they?[7]

David responds (22.09.43):

> it's a pity it exists at all, we Jews have one thing in common with the Negro that is prejudice, reason will break it down one day. One day people will see that a citizen of a country, is not one race, one religion or one colour, but by service to one's country as distinct from Race colour or creed, until that day Negro & Jew must work for good & not ill so that it should be said, 'By their deeds shall ye know them'.

Much of Sylvia and David's attention, however, was on home and domesticity, where reminiscing about the past helped, perhaps, to make the future seem more tangible. Sylvia received a bouquet (25.10.43), and she asks David if he remembers the last occasion he had given her a gift of flowers:

> It was on our third wedding anniversary, while I was in the Home with Ruth. How awkward you seemed with them, you had such an embarrassed air about you almost as if you had been caught doing something 'you didn't oughter.' I do hope, David, that you will be with us to spend the next New Year in peace & plenty.

For David it was the time of the Jewish New Year and the Day of Atonement that brought up memories and some regrets (28.10.43):

> As always with these religious days my thoughts are more than ever with you & Ruth. It seems that religion is a matter of environment & surroundings & one can't be religious away from home, some thing seems lacking, not God, but perhaps goodness that may be the reason.

Still, life went on. There were struggles (28.10.43): Sylvia slapped Ruth after one of her temper tantrums and met her mother-in-law's sharp disapproval, her 'insisting she didn't bring her children up in this way, & that you wouldn't have it either'. Sylvia was confused and yearned for 'a father's firm hand'.

Then (31.10.43) there was a sign of how children could turn high drama into normality:

> As you no doubt know, we have been having occasional short alerts just recently, & when things get a bit lively Fay brings the boys down. They & Ruth make merry with whatever games are about & good time is had by all. I recently bought Ruth a new game during the week – 'Blacking out the moon' – a typical war time game, & also a war time price – 2/3 for what would have been 6d four years ago. When they went to bed after playing the game all evening, Tony said 'I hope we have a warning then we can come down & play your game, Ruth.' To which Ruth enthusiastically agreed. Then again this evening, after an alert of very short though noisy duration, Ruth said with annoyance when the 'all cleared' sounded 'Why doesn't the warning take a long time? – I want to finish the game' I tried to explain what happens when we have a warning & the 'planes come over – 'People get bombed out – like we did – you remember seeing all our furniture in Walthamstow, dirty & broken?' Thoughtfully she asked 'What's in the bombs – is it <u>dust</u>?' – It certainly must have been a very dusty bomb that blitzed 243 – the furniture was in a mess when Ruth last saw it.

Alongside these anecdotes is a reporting of how life is 'so quiet & uneventful' (02.11.43), 'a mere existence – just waiting until this nightmare is over' (04.11.43). Sylvia tells David (02.11.43) how Ruth 'gets rather depressed at times over your lengthy absence, even as I do myself', and she counts how long they have been apart, eighteen months, and how, when she sees other women with their sons and husbands:

> I sometimes think that the fates must have marked me down as one of their unlucky ones … Silly of me really; the news is so bright, & truly optimistic & we must look forward to an early victorious end.

It was, then, good timing for both of them when David announced (4.11.43) his return home on leave, so imminent that the very letter was written on board the ship bringing him home.In it, he is 'excited as hell', and happily anticipates the effect of his news at home:

> Are you laughing or crying? I bet you are shouting the news all over the place, Fay, Betty, Margy & the kids are all round you, or are you collecting your nervous system together?

> I can imagin all these things happening, its because I have lived your thoughts for this occasion over & over again.

> God Bless you sweetheart, the main thing is that I am home & will soon be with you, & then we will have some fun.What is Ruthie saying now?

> Wipe those tears of joy,Your man is home safe & sound.

....

Notes

1   The question of managing sexual tensions was taken seriously by the army. One study of the North African war describes Cairo (which David had visited, describing it as 'one of my most weirdest experiences' (20.08.42)) as busy with 'rancid bars, live shows and urine-and-carbolic-reeking brothels'. This caused such concern that the military set up their own 'authorized brothels … where the Medical Corps handed out condoms and ointments' to the other ranks 'waiting in line to be serviced' (Bierman & Smith, 2002, p.42).

2   These exchanges come over as an intensely individual series of negotiations around their relationship but clearly these were not unique to David and Sylvia. Gardiner (2004) has a fascinating discussion of what two social psychologists of that period described as 'the sex deprivation of separation'. They found that men often told their wives about their infidelities but these were acceptable as 'transient' where the 'circumstances of war exonerated

the husband' (pp.79–80). Nonetheless there were different standards for the wives; affairs were condemned even if the women themselves tended to see these relationships as 'compensatory. While her body might, for a time, be on loan to Jim or Chuck or Stanislav, her heart remained with her husband' (p.81).

3   The Mareth Line was a fortification system on the Libyan–Tunisian border, which was originally constructed by the French before 1939 in order to confront the Italians in Libya, and was subsequently taken, held and occupied by Rommel. This was described as 'so well defended and the terrain so difficult, there was no question of even attempting to make an initial armoured assault' (Bierman & Smith, 2002, p.380). As a response, shortly before midnight on 20 March, the Eighth Army launched the biggest barrage since El Alamein. What followed was a bloody and contradictory battle, but it proved a major victory.

4   David carried with him a *Prayer Book for Jewish Members of H.M Forces* issued with 'the authority of the Chief Rabbi' in 1940. Alongside the normal prayers for, for example, the Sabbath services and the High Holy Days, there is a 'War Prayer' which lamented the 'spirit of perverseness [that] has come over a renowned nation' and 'the shout of the warrior and the roar of the battle [that] resound to the ends of the earth because of the fury of the oppressor'. Consequently it prayed for 'strength and courage and victory on land, sea and in the air' (p.17). There is also a memorial prayer for 'those fallen in battle and for civilian victims of the war' (p 41)

5   This battle confronted the remnants of the German Army Group Africa, 'confined to a small pocket' where 'no territory remained to defend', leading to the surrender of 275,000 Axis soldiers. 'It was the largest capitulation yet imposed by an Allied force ... a grave humiliation for Hitler and a disaster for Mussolini' (Keegan, 1997, p.284). No wonder, given the scale of this victory, that David was so positive.

6   Keegan (1997, p.290) describes this process and how the armies were, indeed, able to secure the Allied line of communications through the Mediterranean to the Middle East.

7   This was not the only example of Jim Crow racism imported into Britain. Gardiner documents the complicated 'pass' procedures set up in the attempt to keep black and white soldiers apart, and the violence (including fatal shootings) when these failed. She also documents that many others shared Sylvia's concerns, 'most of the public … were disturbed by the treatment they saw meted out … they responded to what they saw as the black men's humiliation' (2004, p.483).

Four

1944
A NEW STAGE OF THE WAR

T THIS POINT THERE is a gap in the letters. Until late June, David
is based in the UK, and home leave and telephone calls make
letters superfluous. There are no letters from Sylvia throughout
1944 and we have to assume that David lost them while he was in action.
As a result we only hear Sylvia's voice via David's responses to her
comments and from the memories of those who were with her in Frome,
Somerset, where the Rudoff family had evacuated to escape the bombs
over London. By the end of the year she had been allocated 'Butterfields',
a council home in Walthamstow. David starts this series of letters in
France; here he was busy milking cows and helping deliver babies, and
he also writes of his anger and sorrow when he sees the damage to
homes and people. This increases as he travels into Holland, where he was
involved in Operation Market Garden and then got close to refugees and
the families he was billeted on. As 1944 ends David revisits his political
roots: preparing for the birth of a better world.

• *David: 'Not Very Good News', Heading for France* •

David had his first intimations that things were about to change at the
end of June (29.06.44). He warns Sylvia of the 'not very good news,

strong rumours of an intending move', but he adds (04.07.44) how 'July is a shipping month, July '42 on the way to Egypt, 1943, invasion of Sicily, now France' and he hopes that 1945 will also mean a trip but this time 'with you and baby'.

David talks about his will, reminding Sylvia that everything goes to her, and also states that he 'feels it in his bones' that he will be 'OK'; he will be around 'to look after Terry [the name they had evidently decided upon for their next child, a son] and the others'. This preoccupation with the next generation is a persistent theme, thus he comments (09.07.44) that 'I'm thinking that we shall dispense with all the contraceptions'.

He responds (08.07.45) to Sylvia's worries about him being away and worries in his turn about the Doodlebugs falling on London and how his mother might take the news of him being in France. He intends to write to her 'but am telling them nothing, just say that I am in Scotland' (30.06.44). He encourages Sylvia to take the holiday in Blackpool that she had planned and looks forward to her bringing some rock home for him and he is then relieved at Sylvia's decision to join her family in Frome, away from the bombings.

• *The Family in Frome: 'We Manage!'* •

It is not clear how and why the family decided on Frome, a small town deep in the Somerset countryside, as their place of retreat. Given, as already mentioned, Sylvia's missing letters, it is fortunate that Gloria, a niece of David and Sylvia, is able to share her memories.

Millie, the oldest of the Rudoff children, had a flat over a shop in Cheap Street, a narrow street without traffic and with a water conduit running down the middle. The flat had one especially large room which became like a dormitory, sometimes sleeping her twin daughters Evelyn and Rene; her two nieces, Bunty and Gloria, aged 18 and 15; and Florrie, the long-serving maid. There was a small living room dominated by a dining table around which gathered the immediate household, other visiting family and Jewish American soldiers. One such soldier was Irving, shy and curly haired, who Gloria remembers as looking like the effete Charles Hamilton in *Gone with the Wind*, which caused amusement when he reported going to the annual GWTW Ball in his native Atlanta dressed up as the sexy, macho Rhett Butler. There was Milton, who was keen on Rene and was the butt of endless jokes based on the theme 'A Thousand and One Uses', the advertising slogan for Milton Disinfectant.

Food was endlessly prepared in a tiny adjoining kitchen and Millie, although usually welcoming, could be so provoked by the noise as to shout:'In a minute I AM GOING TO GIVE SUCH A SCREAM!!'

Another Rudoff sister, Belle, subsequently took a shop and flat a few doors away and lived there with her daughter Valerie (aged 11); Jeanie (aged 10), the daughter of another sister, Esther; and Gloria. Gloria remembers Jeanie as 'docile and bewildered'. Belle's husband, Sam, and her daughter, Bunty, came down at weekends and this Bunty regarded as 'a haven of peace and fun' away from the flying bombs in London, with Saturday mornings spent playing records on a wind-up gramophone. There was a weekday rota whereby two of the three girls helped Belle in the kitchen and the third had 'An Easy Evening' with no chores.

The father, Abraham, and 'Auntie Grandpa' also lived over a shop, where Abraham continued his trade of tailoring and selling menswear; on Friday nights he had the grandchildren over to celebrate the Sabbath, lighting the candles and sharing a chicken supper and describing his early years in Britain with an emphasis on his blunders with language and customs. 'Auntie Grandpa' was cheerful in her complaints about the domestic situation, usually ending with the phrase, 'WE MANAGE!'

It is interesting to reflect on how a tiny town in Somerset responded to a family straight from the Jewish East End of London. Certainly Abraham's sales technique was an unusual one, as witnessed by Fay and told to Sylvia, who then passed it on to David (24.08.43):

As you may know, Dad is rather impatient with his customers – with the second-hand goods so scarce & difficult to get, I suppose he feels that customers ought to be grateful to him for supplying them. It appears he had a line in policeman's macs – quite reasonable, & in good condition. A farmer's wife was hesitating over one & queried 'They don't let the rain in, do they?' to which Dad replied 'I've never seen a policeman holding an umbrella.' He further stressed his point by asking the poor bewildered women to hold the mac open & then he picked up a bucket of water &

poured it into the mac. The woman was afraid to let go as the water would have spilt all over the floor, & while Fay could hardly contain herself Dad again pointed out the wonders of the water proofing. After such a thorough demonstration the customer bought the mac.

Meanwhile, Millie was concerned for Sylvia. A letter dated 04.07.44 emphasises that 'I know only too well what you are all going through', but while she wanted Sylvia to leave London and join the family in Frome, it was difficult to find space; 'people are coming from London all day & every day to an already overcrowded area – due to the Bristol, Bath, Portsmouth & Southampton bombings'. However, there was good news because she had been recommended:

a bed sitting room ... front ground floor, most comfortable & pleasant, no cooking facilities as it means going through the other living room. The room includes breakfast for you and Ruth – £1 a week rent ... I think it a God-send, other meals you can have with us and if things ease up in London it can still be a pleasant holiday for the summer weeks.

Millie requests a 'reply <u>per return</u> please' and Sylvia clearly responds because she shortly joins the family in Frome. We know from previous correspondence that Ruth had enjoyed previous holidays there, helping to feed the chickens – 'she stands right in the midst of them scattering their food all around her' – and collecting the eggs (29.08.43). However, while Ruth 'settled down to country life' (31.08.43) it was less successful for Sylvia. Gloria remembers her not being a part of the older generation of her sisters, Millie and Belle, who were then in their mid-forties and came over as 'really old ... seriously burdened with anxieties and a feeling that they were responsible for us', while Sylvia is not yet 30. Gloria actually stopped calling Sylvia 'auntie' and instead developed 'a conspiratorial girlie relationship'. Nevertheless, Sylvia was no longer 'a girl', of course, or part of the younger generation who were full of energy and excitement, alternating trips to Bristol for Communist Party meetings with dances at the nearby American army camps, where 'we were given chewing gum and nylons and told how beautiful we were'. Instead she was in a little bedsit with Ruth at night and with a dominant older sister, Millie, during the day, sharing the very grown-up knowledge, as Gloria puts it, 'that the war was far from over and that there was no certainty that David would come back' let alone Lionel, Ralph, Alf, Sam or indeed that the family who remained in London would survive 'the so-called V1 pilotless bombs and the massively destructive V2 rockets'.

• *France, 1944: 'Going To Finish The Job'* •

David wrote (04.07.44) when he was just a few hours from landing in:

> the country that gave us Liberty, Equality, Fraternity but forgot its meaning, well we've come to free it with the sword, or enslave it with A.M.G.O.T. who knows.

His immediate impressions (08.07.44) were of a country that:

> seems pleasant enough … similar to any of England's especially the south, it's peaceful too except for the continual sounds of guns in the far distance.

He was surprised that the people were fair and very like the English, and he looked forward to learning 'the lingo'. He notices the women (28.08.44) who:

> are very nice and smartly clothed, fashions are very English, they go in perhaps for a bit more colours, vivid ones I mean, they smile prettily.

He also saw the 'shrines and grottoes at nearly every street corner … some beautiful churches' (30.09.44).

For all this fascination, he wanted his life as a soldier to be over. After his period of being based at home – 'I miss my short breaks like Hell' – he muses that 'surely our life cant always be full of hellos and Good byes'.

He asks Sylvia to keep him stocked up with things he will need but the army might be slow to provide. He requests 10/- to be sent in an ordinary letter (29.06.44), some flints and wicks (09.07.44). He receives (30.08.44) £1 from Sylvia's father, 'he's a good old stick', but this embarrasses him, and he protests that he is not in need, and that his average spending is only 5/- a week at the canteen. He had plenty of 'cigs' and was getting soap and toilet stuff from his mother and Vera, his aunt, which was 'O.K. but you can get too much of that'. It was 'coca, sacherine and milk powder' that he was after, and books, mysteries and westerns with names like *The Mystery of the Semi-Nude* and *She Strangled Her Lover* (12.07.44). He got washing powder from Sylvia (04.08.44), which meant he was getting the 'whitest wash', but was missing talcum powder and blades. Having just done some washing, he jokes (15.09.44):

> I'll make a splendid wife … it's surprising how domesticated we all get. I can wash, cook and even darn.

• 'Getting By': Milking Cows, Avoiding Brothels, and the Sights he has seen – 'They Shook Me' •

At this point 'life is cushy' (16.07.44): he went to the baths and 'the flicks', seeing such films as *Hit the Ice* (12.07.44); there were letters to write and those he received caught him up with the family news and he was 'so greatly amused at the twins [his nieces] heart affairs' (20.07.44). After meeting the Jewish padre he planned to go to a Friday night service and hoped to see friends from home there.

To complement his food rations he picked potatoes out of a field, while 'some of the boys have tried milking cows but they wont stand for it' (16.07.44), although they quickly became more proficient (20.07.44):

> One holds the horns while one milks it, my job is to work the tail up and down like a pump. With a little bit of excitement and bother we manage about a pint.

Soon (09.08.44) he and his fellow soldiers were 'living off the land – fowls, geese, pigs … We have got quite attached to one rabbit, a lovely thing called "Compo"', although its cuteness did not save it from going in the pot. On 25 August he continued the details of daily living: chicken and chips for lunch and sheltering in barns when it rained. He slept in his trousers to keep the crease, after all 'you never know when I might be on your door step and I'll want to look my best' (28.04.44). Overall then he was 'fit as a fiddle, pity my energy is directed towards depopulating the world' (04.08.44).

One thing that was:

> out of bounds are the brothels … so that keeps me out of trouble and bully beef does not count for a lot out here … not that I'm looking for that sort of thing.

Instead he looked forward to making up for the lost time in their lives – he so loved Sylvia that 'it does almost hurt' – and, since there were sexual temptations at home as well as abroad, he tells Sylvia 'to look after yourself and "save your self for me"'. His pride comes over in the comment:

> What will Ruth think of it all? bet she is rather pleased that Daddy is going to finish the job, at least catch Rommel, it will be a feather in her cap at least she wont be ashamed of her Father's war record.

He continues: 'if you could only see our strength, it's amazing the air is ours and so is the earth' (16.07.44). Alongside the steady gains in Normandy there was progress on the other front; he looked forward to some 'steady drinking' of vodka to show his 'appreciation of the Russians'. The heavy rain, 'real blighty weather', however, made for slow progress and the army's advance was 'steady plodding', but he muses how, in Germany, 'the rot has set in, it finished this way in the last war and history has a strange way of repeating itself'. He notes (23.07.44) that German bonds have gone up in the hope of an early victory which would mean that the German industrialists:

> wont be in a position to rake it very soon, you see it's only the working class that can really be patriotic.

Then (28.08.44):

> There is plenty of good news … the grand finale will soon be played … Rumania now, Bulgaria next, Hungary after, the rats are leaving … I truly

believe if we never went in for this unconditional surrender and appealed to the Germany people with just peace terms this war would have ceased now and many lives saved. I am not now concerned with the war, let's get it over, by fair means or foul. It's the peace I'm bothered about, it looks as if in the future, the English will have to lose her smugness, the German his arrogance and other nationals their little petty grievances, a common view will have to be found and it wont be found by cutting each other for world markets, or denying countries their freedom, there is a way and people will see it one day, until that day there will be wars and rumours of wars. Don't mind me I just get this way now and again. Things are happening pretty fast and it just makes you think.

Back to his own immediate situation, he comments (09.08.44):[1]

I've seen some sights these days I can tell you, they shook me, names of town and villages you read about, well, they're just rubble and stones, it's a terrible sight, who thinks of war in the future must be mad, as you say human beings are not nice to know these days … the education of Ruth must be thought of, it is from her generation that our hopes must be built.

On his march through the towns he also saw (23.08.44) houses that were still in good condition, rather than just rubble and destruction. As well, he enjoyed the impact of 'people standing along the side walks cheering and throwing flowers and waving French and English flags', plus the creature comforts of lots of fruit and cider. He took the opportunity, when going to some municipal baths, to enjoy the swimming, hot showers and music, and also to 'get by' with 'the lingo' using 'a mixture of their own German and crude Yiddish' (10.09.44). This marks the beginning of his fraternisations which were to become such a vital part of his wartime experiences.

• *David Apologising: 'I Didn't Have Any Choice'* •

David, in the midst of this, had to manage the serious concerns, distress even, expressed in Sylvia's letters. He apologises for going away, adding 'I didn't have any choice' (08.07.44). He detects (24.07.44) Sylvia's 'coldness',

June 13th 1943

AIR MAIL
LETTER CARD
IF ANYTHING IS ENCLOSED THIS CARD
WILL BE SENT BY ORDINARY MAIL

MRS. S. WEINSTEIN
31, WOODFORD AVE
ILFORD
ESSEX
ENGLAND

Received:— June 23rd 1943
WHEN FOLDED THE LETTER CARD MUST CONFORM IN SIZE AND SHAPE
THE BLUE BORDER WITHIN WHICH THE ADDRESS ONLY MUST BE WRITTEN

191

ushy, the future, well that is
a matter of 1Mosabtai, if I said
anything else, I would be
detained under regulation 18b +
I would not want "Healy to
intern one of his best friends
so the next best thing to do is
talk about the weather.

It is now getting too hot
to be comfortable, + ice cream
sodas are not now available
so one must grin + bear it.

The news is good + very
promising for the future. Italy
like giving up already, we
are all hearing raids + her
morale will be smashed up.
Germany must be very
worried though she has very
strong coastal defences,
certainly not defence in
depth so soon as a landing

will be made + maintained. the
peoples in all the occupied countries
will be with us, + Germany will
not be able to fight back. that
is a strong army on its front +
an army of saboteurs at its rear.
which doesn't mine. points only
to one thing. Victory this year
+ your beloved husband being
home soon.

Well sweetheart mine shall
close now, give my love to
all at Woodford, my bestest
love to you + Ruthie.

God Bless
Yours Ever
David

X for You
X for Ruth

Surabaya
June 13th 1943

Darl Weinstein
1101886. B.T.C.
R101/124 Field
M.E.F.

My dearest Sylvia

Not heard from a
for at least five days, whats be
not what I blame you, but mail
for the last week has been very
browsy, perhaps shall get some
mail to-night, I hope so.

I'm seeing quite a lot of Ra
he is only a couple of hundred
yds away from me, he looks rel
+ fit, + as you can imagine we
have lots to tell each other.

I hope by this time you have had
some of my leave snaps. I hope
you liked them.

There is not a lot to write
about these days. the past is
gone + its deeds has made
history, the present, well thats

BY AIR MAIL

AIR LETTER

IF ANYTHING IS ENCLOSED
THIS LETTER WILL BE SENT
BY ORDINARY MAIL

ILFORD ESSEX 9.45AM 22 FEB 1943

1101886 GNR. D. WEINSTEIN
441/124th FIELD REGT.
E. TROOP   R.A
MIDDLE EAST
FORCES

Second fold here

To open cut here

name and address:-
...L Weinstein
31 Woodford Ave,
Ilford, Essex
ENGLAND

No. 96   Saturday — Feb. 20th 1943

David dearest,

I wrote you an airgraph on Thursday (which you have, no doubt, had long ago) to let you know that I had at last received the various photos mailed on Sept 6th. I also had a second letter by the same post (Sept 30th) & it was grand having two nice long letters to read.

Today, however, I was really most surprised to receive yet another airmail letter, containing to my great joy, another of those photographs of the three of us — similar to the one I received so badly burnt on Jan. 20th. This letter was dated Nov. 29th — the damaged one was Nov. 30th. Strange how the deliveries varied so greatly. — Now, of course, I can understand what you meant in that burnt letter when you said you were sending me "another of those photos". I'm so glad you did send them separately — they may have all been destroyed in that damaged letter. The box of Turkish Delight

hasn't yet arrived, but will be none-the-less welcome when it does. Jay says you should have sent three boxes, just in case a couple should go astray as in the case of the photos (should a second photo turn up, I shall pass it on as requested — to Mother I guess. — Wish you had been able to send six of yourother — I should have liked to send Dad one too.)

I was very interested by your description of the Palestinian visits. — I think I'd like to visit Palestine some day- if is as you say, a youthful nation; healthy, happy, virile & contented — confident of what they are building!

Glad to note that you have had a wireless lent you, & that you are all able to listen in to some programmes. I didn't realise that you were as much as two hours ahead of British time — does that mean that when I am saying "goodnight" to you so faithfully every night at 10½, that you are soundly asleep out there, being midnight? —

I'm glad you wrote a nice

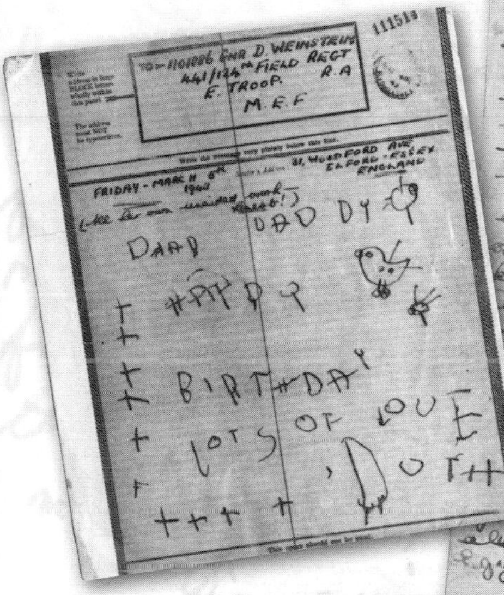

Sunday
June 13th 1943

To — 1101886 Gnr D. Weinstein
441/124th Field Regt
R.A.
E. Troop
M.E.F.

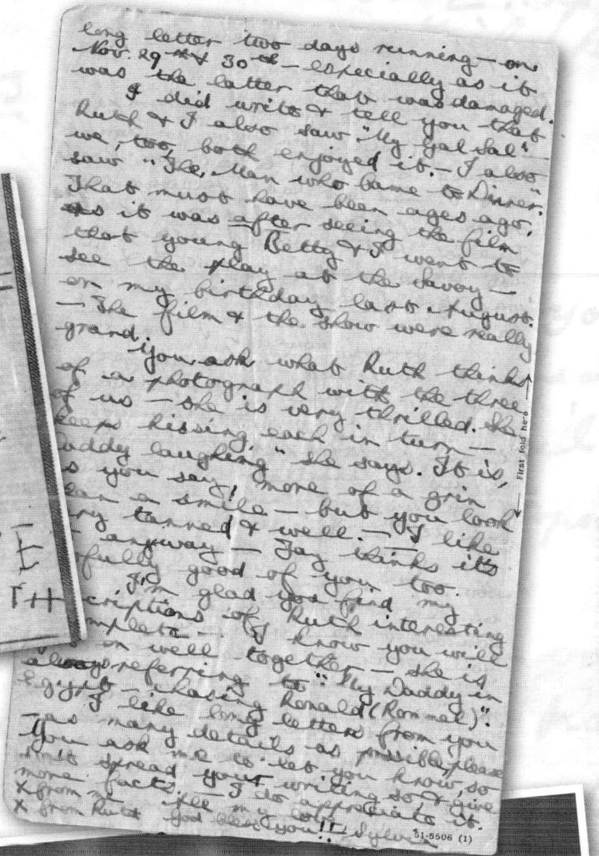

31, Wanstead Ave,
Ilford Essex
ENGLAND

FRIDAY - MARCH 5th 1943

DADDY   DADDY

HAPPY

BIRTHDAY

LOTS OF LOVE

DOT

I

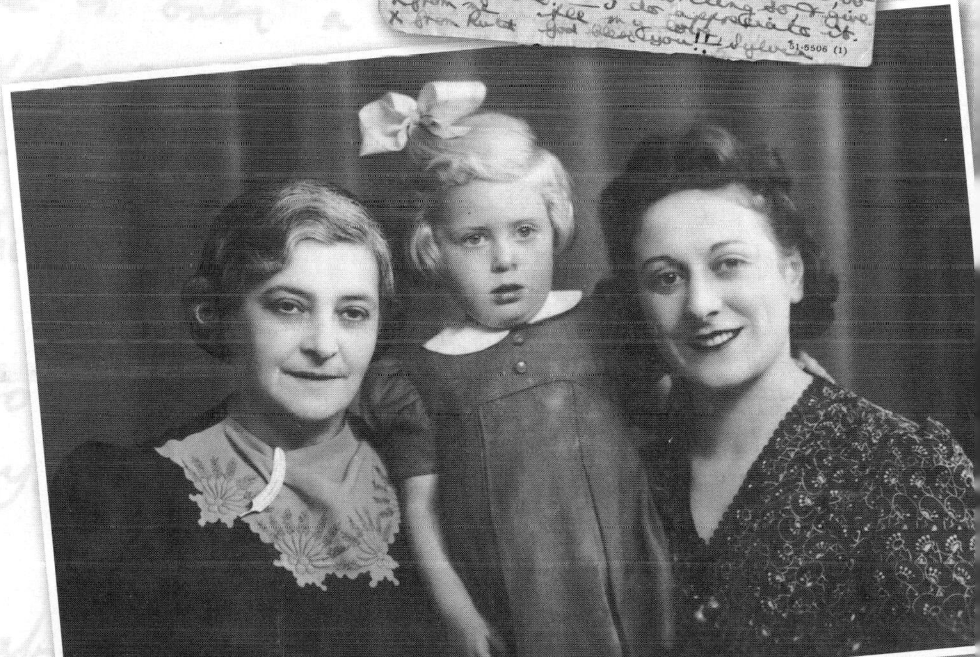

To Sylvia
With love
David

2

WAR DAMAGE ACT 1943 (PART II) - PRIVATE CHATTELS SCHEME

	The final amount payable as shown on the Payable Order is arrived at as follows :—	
	PAYABLE ORDER No.	£ S. D.

A Payable Order (the yellow card) is enclosed in settlement of the War Damage Private Chattels claim of which particulars are given on the Order. From the amount of the assessment, advance payments (if any) made by the Assistance Board, Customs and Excise Department, Board of Trade, or Local Authorities have been deducted ; and where the damage occurred before 1st May, 1941, on which date the Private Chattels Scheme came into force, the amount chargeable in lieu of insurance premium has been deducted as follows :—

Nil on first £300 of the assessment ;
1½% on the next £1,700 ;
1¾% on the next £1,000 ;
2% on the next £7,000.

The Payable Order may be passed through a bank or paid into an account in the Post Office Savings Bank, a Trustee Savings Bank, or the Birmingham Municipal Savings Bank. It cannot be cashed at a Post Office.

If you have no bank account, payment may be obtained through a third person (for example, a friend or tradesman) who is willing to pass the Payable Order through his bank for you.

Your particular attention is called to the enclosed Government leaflet about investment in National Savings.

A statement is also enclosed (the pink card) showing the amount of income tax that has been deducted from the interest. This statement will enable those claimants who are not liable to tax at the standard rate to apply to their Tax Officer for a refund of the tax, in whole or in part.

Supplementary payments are made only in respect of claims assessed at more than £25 and less than £1,200 for war damage which occurred before the end of 1941, where the claims were not wholly paid up by the end of that year. Supplementary payments are calculated on the amount of the assessment as follows :—

Assessments exceeding £25 but not exceeding £350 - 50 per cent of the assessment
Assessments exceeding £350 but not exceeding £762/10/0 - a flat increase of £175
Assessments exceeding £762/10/0 but not exceeding £1,200 - two-fifths of the difference between the assessment and £1,200

It is not necessary to acknowledge the receipt of the Payable Order.

Issued by THE BOARD OF TRADE (OP/1)
JERSEY ROAD, OSTERLEY, ISLEWORTH, MIDDLESEX

Z 292274		249. 0. 0	AMOUNT OF ASSESSMENT OUTSTANDING.
		38.16. 4	ADD INTEREST ON ABOVE AMOUNT (IT IS NOT PAYABLE IN ADVANCE), AT 2½% PER ANNUM FROM DATE OF DAMAGE TO DATE OF PAYABLE ORDER.
The Standard Rate in the £ of Tax that has been deducted is :— S. D. 9 0		17. 9. 4	DEDUCT INCOME TAX ON THE INTEREST AT THE CURRENT STANDARD RATE.
		129.10. 0	ADD SUPPLEMENTARY PAYMENT (IF ANY).
	£	399. 17. 0	NET AMOUNT PAYABLE.

Dining room included: (clock + picture)

electric light fitting	£3	0 0
four cushions	2	0 0
pair curtains two × fittings 7/6	1-17-6	
½ tea service completely broken	1-2-6	
carpet damaged	15	0
	£9·5·0	

Bedroom included:—

two pairs curtains	£3	0 0
window fittings	15	0
cut glass dressing table set ×6	1-10-0	
ornaments	1-1-0	
personal trinkets & watch	5-0-0	
personal clothes & effects	30-0-0	
eiderdown damaged torn + soiled (2 pairs)	3-0-0	
	£45-15-0	

Bathroom fittings:
electric fitting broken completely destroyed
medicine cabinet + fittings ... 7-8-0
bath stool containing linen ... 12-6
two bath towels ... 1-0-0
... 2-17-6

Stair carpet damaged ... £2-0-0

Shop parlour fittings
rug + arm chair £1-10-0 ... 2-0-0
writing desk destroyed ... 3-0-0
All furniture chipped + requiring
repolishing
Shop fittings remaining all fixtures
shelves, counters, window fittings
electric light fitting ...

Then lives, electric wiring—landlord's claim

large glass counter (made by own carpenter)		
large glass hanging wall + show case	£5-0	
mirror ″ ″ (glass)	£15	
glass oval inside window (bought)	£10	
″ shelves	£5	
lamp + shades (inside) plots	£5	
″ ″ (outside) window	£15	
Blinds (two) approx.	£5	
	£15	
	£12·0	
Stands + brackets + fitments		
	£15	
	1·35	

Lino — too badly damaged to be removed

(Lino)

Sitting room furniture included:—

one fireside chair completely destroyed	£2-0-0	
second spoilt by water	£6-0-0	
dining table badly burned	£5-0-0	
four chairs damaged	£2-0-0	
bookcase ″ several books destroyed	£3-0-0	
″ destroyed	£1-0-0	
wireless set destroyed	£12-0-0	
glassware broken	3-0-0	
clock	1-1-0	
mirror	10-0	
2 cushions destroyed	9-0-0	
baby's pram	4-0-0	
carpet + bedding ×5 including rugs	1-0-0	
complete wardrobe	2-0-0	
highchair damaged	4-7-0	
electric fittings destroyed		
two rugs destroyed		
curtains ×5 + fittings 10/	£66-3-0	

Scullery fittings included:—

tea service broken	5-0-0	
½ dinner service	15-0	
½ port dinner service	3-0-0	
boiling stove also chipped burnt	1-0-0	
washing accessories completely destroyed	15-0	
kitchen clock broken	15-0	
curtains destroyed + fittings 5/	£8-15-0	

3

4

5

6

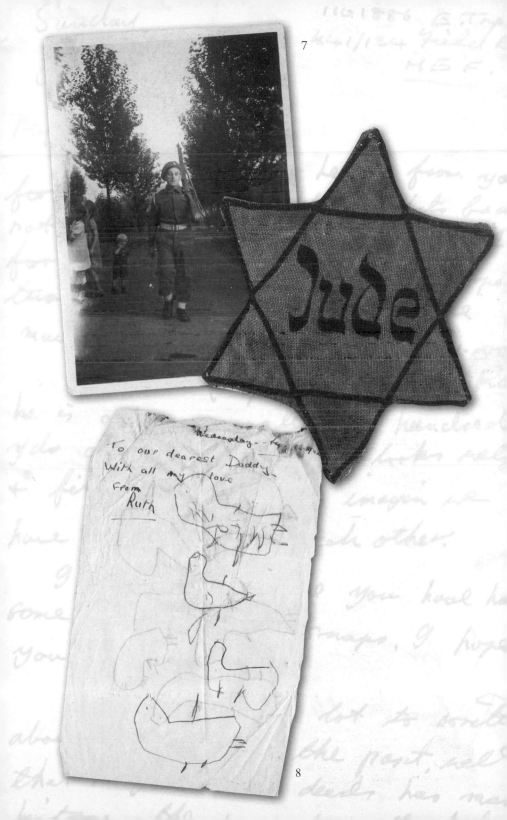

7

8

To our dearest Daddy
With all my love
from
Ruth

Wednesday

The **noble** and pure friendship also may mean absently very much; to feel that also remote one's thought of, enlarges and doubles the own existence

Friedrich von Schiller.

In memory of my English colleague.

It seldom happens in life to meet men worthy of a dedication. In you my dear English colleague Weinstein, I found such one.

You always had an ear for the matters we must endure in Germany.

Your attitude was collegial, moving me very deeply in my heart. Filled in our destiny, we exchanged psychical suffering each other and quieted by the way, the war, went, we strong the balance.

As I am unable to express my thank in an other way, please take as a sign of my thank this dedication with you into your home with the certainity that you mean much for me and that you have good memory in me.

I wish you further on fortune and contentment in the circle of your family.

Your colleague

Ludwig Müller

Germany, Bochum
in December 1945.

9

10

her 'crib' at his ending a letter 'yours always', and he guesses this is because
she had not heard from him. He urges Sylvia not to regret what failed to
happen in July: 'it's cushy when it does happen' (which suggests her not
getting pregnant). Then (12.08.44) he apologises again when an attempt
to make a joke just leaves her feeling 'narked'. In the same letter he
responds to some earlier failure of communication concerning a problem
he had wanted to share:

> I felt pretty bad about it and just wanted to know how you felt. If we
> had been together and living normally it would have been a topic of a
> conversation by the fire side … Any way, enough said, shan't tell you a thing
> about them again.

On 23 August, Sylvia's upset was not with him:

> So sorry you felt like writing as you did and the pity of it is that there is not
> much I can do about it but now perhaps Thursday is over you and Mother
> are not feeling so bad.

He urges her not to be cynical, 'you'll find good in all people', and adds
that 'out here' there is 'super optimism and we ought to know', but he adds:

> still sweetheart mine I understand your point of view perfectly and if you
> ever want to unburden yourself well I'm here for you to write.

Ruth also features in the letters. On 13 August he sent her a big 'X' 'for
writing me such a nice letter and drawings' and on 21 August he was
sad that such 'a little mite' might have to have her tonsils out. He shares
Sylvia's worries about whether this is the right thing to do but says that it
has to be Sylvia's decision, and hers alone. Sylvia, being in Frome, brought
him news of the wider family. His niece, Gloria, was busy sketching and he
looked forward to seeing these pictures and notes his reaction (07.09.44)
to an example of her literary work.

> Certainly I enjoyed that bit of pornographic literature, but now I've got
> a different picture of my virtuous nieces, instead I can see Gloria secretly

typing and the others giggling over indecent literature. I'd like to exert an uncle's authority and give them all a good spanking, but then I forgot that I was young too, but I thought girls who were modern would scorn such crude stuff.

But please tell them, in case they get the wrong impression, that Love and Sex are two great emotions. We fickle with them, they then become just cheap sensation. We know dont we darling. You can quote me on that. I think that last paragraph is a bit of a masterpiece.

In the same letter he describes how the French are so 'wildly enthusiastic … [that] I've been offered woman in nearly every town'.

As time goes on his thoughts about home become more specific: he reminds Sylvia 'to keep up the insurances' and considers becoming a commercial traveller once the war is over. He looks forward to the Jewish New Year in 1945 and hopes that 'Ruth will have a young brother to show off in shool [synagogue]'. He states that he will be done with soldiering once the 'German war' is over and promises that he would 'go to prison first rather than go to India. I've seen enough and done more than my share' (11.09.44).

A Happy New Year, 'A Hive of Activity' Moving on From France, Through Belgium and into the Netherlands

With the Jewish festivals pending, David wishes his family (18.09.44) 'a happy new year and well over the fast'. David's 'eruv yom tov' was actually:

a hive of activity. the air vibrated with our air craft and the earth trembled with the bark of our guns. It certainly was a great battle, today it is quite if not peaceful. My thoughts are naturally full of what might have been had the world been sane, so it's a strange New Year celebrating I'm doing, still if it is going to ensure the peace of the world for ever, then it's a good job I'm doing … Since we first landed except for an odd day or two have been in action all the time and this included chasing, don't get me wrong its all been really pleasant and no time have I been in danger, that is close enough,

the stray shell or so you will always come up against, and you just unlucky
… for the operation we've been on, our casualties have been very light,
nobody killed about 10 wounded and that out of 150 men. We've just been
very lucky and I think our luck will hold.

Moving on through and deeper into Europe felt to him like 'one last fling'
and he became increasingly impatient for the war to end. He calculated
when he might get his discharge and hoped to be 'one of the first out'
(11.09.44), since every two months of war service counted as a year, which
added up to fifty-six, and he had been told that all those with a total of
over fifty would get immediate release. With his discharge would come
two months' money, including his overseas service, which would amount
to nearly three months' holiday with pay. Taking into consideration his
post-war credits and gratuity he would 'be coming home with a wad
of notes'. While David was 'dry enough' under a tarpaulin sheet, he
was 'praying hard that it will be over before the winter sets in'. He also
acknowledged that 'it will take years to get the army system out of me'
(20.09.44) and he commented that, given the speed of the advance:

> when we capture places we rumble thro at 40 miles an hour … most likely
> … in the early hours of the morning or in darkness while the Base blokes
> … reep the benefits of our advances and big Towns.

He had earlier (10.09.44) been critical of 'Base blokes' with their quick
promotions These, David explains, were:

> pretty easy its what we call protection stripes they come up with the rations,
> not being nasty but believe me there is no honour attached to it.

Sylvia's nephew, Lionel, was also a target. He had been training pilots in
Canada where he had taken a wife, but David had heard that Lionel could
get caught up in:

> the Jap side of the business … well that wont do him any harm remember
> that photo taken of him and Millie [Lionel's mother] wrote 'one of the
> few' etc. etc., well its about time he did some thing, he can't have it all

bees and honey, not that he'll do much, he is coming back just at the right time.

Another factor in the army's fast progress was that getting the mail to the troops was not the first priority, so when it did catch up with them, David revelled in the backlog. He received not just letters but also 'a beauty of a lighter … the talk of the whole camp'. He was not worried that Sylvia got it via 'a Yanky' – she was 'above suspicion'. He was also relieved that Ruth was OK:

> I was really touched about her wanting my small photograph to take with her … I feel that also essential to my life is to be suddenly confronted with my daughter wanting to climb on me and give me one of those wet kisses and say I love you daddy, it is one of the joys of life … I had to laugh quite loud at that rude dream of hers. It must have shocked her, so she wants to know some thing about 'be married' well please God when the time comes I hope she is 'be married' as happy as we two.

Now in the Netherlands, he observed that, apart from the children and the men at work wearing clogs, 'clothes are very modern' and the women 'are beautiful in a heavy sort of way'. Again his 'crude Yiddish' combined with 'their own German' allowed David to get by with the local people and he visited the municipal baths where he enjoyed the swimming, hot showers and music, but there were limitations:

> the Dutch are not so demonstrative as the Belgiums or the French but then the war is not passing them so quickly … there is no difference in the working classes in any part of the world except for differences in their degree of poverty.

Earlier (10.09.44) he noted that with Bulgaria now an ally it made:

> a headache for those who's job it will be to reconstruct national boundaries or will it solve itself by becomming more Soviets of the U.S.S.R.

• *Operation Market Garden: David is 'One of those Fighting Men'* •

The fighting caught up with David. He started with the hint that he was having (23.09.44) 'a pretty busy time', then followed this up (30.09.44) with 'the true story':

> You must know by the papers that we advanced quickly along one road, well it was a bit risky (incidently I was with the forward elements) well Jerry cut the road behind us, that lasted for a few days, then we crossed a bridge and he blew that up, so supplies weren't too good, so you had a right to be worried, but now everything is O.K.

Enclosed with this letter was a news cutting headlined: 'Kept open road for British in Holland'. It tells the story of the American 101st Airborne Division, which, with an attached group of British tanks, moved to secure vital bridges and take the first major city of Eindhoven. This is described as 'a desperate all-out attempt' by the Germans to cut off 'thousands of British vehicles, armour and troops [that] had poured through for nearly four days' from 23 September for thirty-six hours, but it was successfully fought off with 4,000 prisoners taken.

Subsequently (11.10.44) David refers to seeing off the:

> 'Arnhem boys' – a sorry affair but it made it possible to hold the Nymejam bridge head which incidently I was a part of ... one of those fighting men ... even Tommy's of other units are proud to shake hands with you.

It was not until 3 April 1945 that he was he able to tell Sylvia another side to this battle, admitting that:

> if I'd stayed much longer in that Nigmeyan area I'm sure I would have broken down, I nearly reached breaking point when we were shelled out of two positions in one day and lost three killed and six wounded.

This battle was Operation Market Garden.[2]

• *David: 'Making your own Comforts'* •

With the fighting on hold, David (03.10.44) searched out some foreign money to send home to Ruth and got busy:

> cutting up some of the fur skins that Jerry left behind, I say fur, it must be very poor rabbit skin, the lads are busy sowing them into jerkins, they are rather crude, but they'll do for winter wear. It's a grand life, you learn to make your own comforts, role on the day when the only comfort and warmth I'll want will be in your arms.

As for the countryside, he found:

> nothing beautiful … it is flat as a pancake, ditches all over the show and plenty of mud, the bright spot being the apples and pears are a delight to eat, even what women we see, are drab and uninteresting.

The towns, however, were more interesting (11.10.44). Whereas the French towns struck him as:

> terrible … dirty and narrow streets, houses that looked a hundred years old … Belgium and Holland are quite different, they can teach us a lesson in Town planning, with roads, avenues of trees giving shade, houses with (illegible) windows and an atmosphere that smells of cleaniless and health. This part of Holland is pretty badly hit and the refugee problem is pretty tragic, I think I'm seeing the worst side of war this time and believe me it some times leaves me in a rotten frame of mind.

He then had leave in Brussels, staying in the Hotel des Colonies, which 'is a real posh joint' with meals served by waiters in white jackets, music at every meal and flowers on the table. Just before writing his letter (16.10.44) he had 'a real slipper bath' and on his bed was 'the joy' of beautiful white sheets. It was also all for free, and such lavish treatment from the army had quite shaken him. The next day he expected to be woken with an early morning cup of tea and then to go shopping, although everything looked dear, and to get some photos taken. The shops were fully stocked and there were plenty of people and transport. It was 'a real capital, wide streets and beautiful'. He drank expensive champagne at Maxim's Bar, 'just like you see on films, a small floor for dancing, crooners and turns'.

His next letter (17.10.10) continues the theme: his leave was 'sumptious … [with] plenty to eat, fresh fruit and cigars served after your dinner'. He enjoyed drinking beer in the cafés, the ices, the music and cabaret turns, but it was 'all too short' and he would soon 'be back to earth again'. He didn't mind, however, as he had had a rest and a break and the chance to shop: a broach for Sylvia, a bracelet for Ruth, 'little gifts' that he could only post when he got back to his unit.

While in Brussels (24.10.44):

> I was stopped three times by woman of the night all in fur coats, well I wasnt going to help to buy them another … girls who had never been touched before and woman who couldn't remember when they were first touched, they had been so long at it. I do see the seemy side of life … I read and heard of these things but now I know.

Returning to camp, he writes (20.10.44):

> I've seen graves in the wildnes of the desert, in the vine-yards of Sicily, and now in the by-ways and ditches of the continent all standing there – a silent contribution to some poor Mother's war effort, they seem to mock you – what would they say if they could only speak – they accuse all of us – a fine mess we've made of things and what is remembered of them? but some-where some-one sheds a silent tear … I've got this off my chest, I feel a lot better now, Bless you my darling, you're the only one I can write like this to.

Nonetheless he was in the best of health: 'I seem to thrive on this kind of life … I really must be tough', he was 'keeping well and warm', aided (30.10.44) by his helping to build a 'super duper' underground dugout, 9ft x 7ft, 1½ft deep and made safe inside by thick pieces of wood so that the sides did not collapse in, and with bags of earth on top. There was a bricked floor and a fireplace complete with chimney, 'warm and comfy' and wanting only some pictures of pin-up girls that Sylvia had promised to send him: 'it will make real dandy wall paper.' However, he was only protected fully while in the dugout so he asks Sylvia (01.11.44) to send him some Wellington boots. He had been issued a pair but only had half ownership of them, 'they have to handed over to the guy who takes over when I go off duty'.

His other creature comforts included cash sent by Belle, another sister-in-law, although he was far from poor; a new wage rise back-dated to September meant he could actually send some money back home to help the holiday bank book get 'nice and fat'. He received some letters that told him that Ruth now had plaits and looked charming, and 'talks yiddish like a natural'. He was also pleased that Butterfields (the council home in Walthamstow to which he would be returning) was still standing: 'it's one room for food, one recreation, another for procreation its "just the job"'. He enjoyed the magazines that Sylvia had sent, and tells how:

> some of the lads get 'Womens Own' and have great fun with the problem page. One of the lads suffers from pimples … he's going to write to her, the reply we expect, will be that once he's begun his periods they will go, he is only a youngster, only 19.

There was also an obligatory lecture from the padre about non-fraternisation with 'Jerry'. David did not appreciate being told how to be with the people he could meet and he quotes, 'if thine enemy hunger and thirst give him food and drink' (30.10.44).

• Looking For 'A Nitch': With the Refugee Families and Reflecting on his Life at Home •

David put this principle into practice through his involvement with some of the refugees. He had previously (30.10.44) told Sylvia about seeing refugees 'living in stables and barns, expected mothers, old and young living like cattle'. Now he had taken the opportunity of getting involved, especially with one family: 'we are so friendly now, that we join in their joys and sorrows.' He witnessed (24.11.44) the death of 'a sweet old lady of 83' and the birth of a baby boy in a cellar. He exclaims, 'what a world.' In the nine weeks that he and his soldier friends knew this mother and child 'we laughed and cried together' and they looked through their packs to see what gifts they could give. Sylvia also sent some baby clothes. 'Believe me were now part and parcel of village life.' He lists the names of a group of girls aged 3 to 11 who came up to camp when the canteen had been and there were chocolates around, and they were 'kissing and cuddling you, they are artful like all children, they pronounce my name Daavid'. He talks (05.11.44) of:

> the debt I have to pay in my own mind, I shall try to make this world a better place to live in … I know you'll help me in this resolve, with you behind me I shall go all the way.

Sylvia was evidently concerned about whether, after all this, he would ever settle back behind a counter in a small shop. He admits (08.11.44) that he might be tempted by 'the dole, just signing the dotted line for my pay', but if he had a big family:

> I say it with reluctance I must do some sort of work to keep them, we'll see, they'll be a nitch for me somewhere in this world of ours.

He was nostalgic for this time the previous year when he had been stationed in the UK and able to phone every day and with regular leave. In his next letter (11.11.44) he sustained this personal focus on Sylvia, pleased that she had received his present of perfume, which he wanted her to know cost 'about 22/-' and had come from pre-war Paris. He responds to Sylvia's reminder of Torquay in 1937 and matches her memory with more of his own:

> the motor boat ride back from Babbican, just two of us alone … those little ducks … those buns with cream and tea … a water proof apron … great days … So the urge is still as strong as ever, well it's been pretty strong with me too, don't worry soon I'll be giving you all the satisfaction in the world, other wise I'm not the sort the man I used to be, and it will give the greatest of pleasure.

Then bad weather prevented any letters reaching him, weather which was 'lousy with a capital L' and left him with 'mud up to your ankles and over', along with 'utter boredom, sleeping continually in one's clothes', so he was 'reaching a stage of complete browned off-ness'. Subsequently (24.11.44) David describes the rain flooding rats out of their homes in the dykes: 'we've killed seven and the fight is not over yet'. He knew he should not write like this – Sylvia had her own troubles – 'but to-day I can't just put down an OK, feeling cheerful, am far from it'. Whereas some had 'cushy billets' in civilian houses that had been requisitioned, this was not so for soldiers like him because 'our guns must be in the open so naturally we are more exposed to the elements'. He did, however, acknowledge that he was better off than 'the P.B.I (poor bloody infantry)'.

Learning that Churchill anticipated the war being over by the spring or summer of 1945, David did not envisage being in the Army of Occupation or in any further fighting. He ends with his usual sort of sentence: 'Bestest love to you and Ruth. Regards to all. Yours always, David' and two big "X"s.'

Subsequently (15.11.44) he apologises for the earlier 'rotten letter'; he had been cheered by twelve pages from Sylvia, expressing her 'news love and affection … Bless you'. This included the story of Ruth learning a song that he hoped to sing with her one day and he liked the drawings he had been sent: 'she shows promise of opening up a completely new school of art, futuristic is hardly the word for it.'

Missing Ruth was a constant hurt. He asks (24.11.44) for a photo of her: 'she must be growing up fast and I don't want to lose track of her' and in a second letter with the same postmark he enjoys Sylvia's stories about her and is 'narked' to be missing her progress.

In November (16.11.44) he requested some nude pin-ups which:

> always seem to go down well, we study them then criticise and make suggestions, it provides a topic for the whole evening.

Another way of passing time and avoiding boredom were quizzes and spelling bees, which were organised via the loudspeaker units on each of the guns and the tannoy, which was linked up to the command post so that:

while sitting in front of the fire in our dug out the order is 'get your paper and pencil out and here goes'.

As he approached this fourth anniversary as a soldier he reflected on how he had always 'hated uniformity in everything', but while previously it had been all theory, if he hated it still 'it wont be a question of talking thro my hat'. On the other hand, he did value the army for the opportunity to meet all the 'grand lads from all the corners of England'.

He then turns to his anger about the relief fund for 18B detainees[3] and he promises that once he has 'finished sorting out the filthy type of German Fascism I shall start on the English variety'.

· *'Getting Quite Continental': Contrasting Billets* ·

As Christmas approached he had some leave, which provided a respite from the rats and the rain, and also gave him a chance to get closer to the lives of the people.

He was billeted (01.12.44) in a small village, with the family of the local school's headmaster. He shared a room and a 'good old fashioned double bed' with a fellow soldier and he relished being able to write his letter (03.12.44) 'sitting at the kitchen table in front of the fire with the radio playing'. He was able to ignore the rain: 'I've got four walls to protect me from the elements.' He also had a vantage point from which to observe this traditional setting where the man was very much the head of the family:

> like a King on his throne, he sits down to his meals, skull cap on, napkin hanging from his collar and his wife and daughters dance attendance on him, he is a decent old stick, he and I together are teaching each other our languages, it's quite a game, last night it was past 12 o'clock when I got to bed. I always get early morning coffee and biscuits, its nice to be made a fuss of, they are very religious, the girls have never seen either a film or a play, it is 'verboten' they are Catholics.

He was introduced (05.12.44) to a new dish, an omelette fried with slices of apple and plenty of sugar, and also (07.12.04) coffee without sugar or milk. David observed, with some satisfaction, that it seemed that 'I'm getting quite continental'. He went to the cinema and saw *The Desert Song*, enjoying a civic reception for the soldiers, complete with national songs by the children, and a march past. He was less impressed with the weak beer. When he left (14.12.44) this 'nice little village and the good family ... they were all on the point of crying ... I too was very sorry'.

Some months later (11.04.45), prompted by a letter from them, he reminisces about this family. The 18-year-old was, apparently, 'broken hearted' and David recalls how he befriended and used:

> to make love to her and chip her in my most peculiar Dutch, I sang her love ballads and in order to reach my top notes I used to climb on the table and then there were roars of laughter.

His new billet was rather different, a larger town which meant 'more life, amusements, pictures and brothels, every thing a soldier desires'. There was also ice cream and pasties, albeit 'at fancy prices', and:

> a thriving black market ... the poor find living pretty deadly, still it existed before we liberated them but we ought to try to stop it ... Our billets, though still caring, is not in the same class, nice people but definitely working class, not that I'm snobbish, but for comfort our last place was heaps better.

A surprise leave in Brussels provided a chance to buy expensive stockings for Sylvia, a dolly and some picture bricks for Ruth and perfume for other family members: Doris, Betty, Mother and Vera. However, this shopping opportunity also starkly illustrates (13.01.45) how all 'the wealth and good food on display' betrays the lack of any 'semblance at all that a war exists'. This was far from being:

> typical of ordinary life in Belgium ... in the working class areas food and clothing are rationed leaving people on the poverty line and there is a shortage of coal so heating is only used sparingly for cooking – just one hour a day – with people going to bed early to keep warm. But the black market provides any thing but at a price.

On the other hand, housing was cheap, 5/- rents for ordinary workers, while 'posher' accommodation was £1. There were also other deprivations. He was presently billeted with a young mother of about 30 with a 6-year-old child; since her husband had been taken to work in Germany in May 1940 she had received just one letter and she now had no idea where he was.

Back in his regiment there were other disruptions to be faced. Having got as 'thick as thieves' with old friends (17.12.44), the regiment was being split up, for reasons that he could not explain in the letter. He tried to be positive: he was (21.12.44) missing 'the old faces but expecting to be making new friends soon'. On top of this, mail was disrupted and he was 'lost without them [letters]'. He was then left looking forward to his next leave and hoping that it 'will be the last parting for both of us'.

• *As 1944 Ends David Remembers his Political Roots: Preparing for 'The Birth of a Better World'* •

In the meantime there was an unseasonable season to survive. For all the promise of the Christmas dinner (24.12.44), 'Turkey (tinned), pudding fresh fruit sweets and extra ration of cigs and not forgetting 2 bottles of Blighty beer', this could not prevent the whole event being 'miserable', with the men cursing the war 'and all those that were guilty of fermenting it and they weren't all Germans' (26.12.44). His mood had been darkened (24.11.44) by press reports suggesting that V1s and V2s would be the weapon of the future and those assuming that wars were 'part and parcel of mankind'. In contrast (27.11.44), his belief was that 'this world has had labour pains too long now, perhaps the birth of a better world is not far off'. The nature of that 'better world' was then challenged, however, in a letter from his 15-year-old niece, Gloria. He expresses his exasperation (10.12.44) at her attempt to convert him:

> the cheek of these kids, you can tell her that I was reading Karl Marx when she was still sucking at her mother's breast, also that I've long left behind that feeling of head in the sky that young people have, practical politics is my game now, something that the CP can never have ... I wonder what the

CP would do with out their shepherd 'Joe'? Strange that the kids have gone all Red with their Folks blessing too. I'm most surprised.

Later (30.12.44) he acknowledges that 'I like her youthful enthusiasm, it's all to the good', while a letter from Phil, his old friend and comrade from his ILP days, then in the Communist Party, provokes David's comment:

> he like me, thinks the war militarily is going good, but politically it stinks, it looks as if we both will have to get in to the thick of things and see if we can't straighten out a few problems as we fighting men see it.

A further letter from Gloria (13.01.45), who was apparently 'het up' because he called her 'a kid', provokes him into wanting to remind his family (and himself perhaps) of his 'past achievements in politics':

> I joined the I.L.P at 14 ½ yrs of age. Executive member of the Finsbury Labour Party, chairman of the local I.L.P. and platform speaker at 15. Shop steward and London committee member of the union at 17 ½. Spoke on the same platform as the great Tom Mann, believe me no mean record.

A major preoccupation was to get some leave; indeed, he writes to the troop commander 'to help shift things' and his thoughts turn increasingly toward home. The Christmas Eve letter (24.12.44) is especially eloquent:

> May God take all the darkness of the last five years and give you light for ever and Ruth and I share it with you and rejoyce in its blessings. I love you such a lot and miss you so much too much of my life has been spent from you, its like a scholar without his books, a magician without his wand … I'm just a mere number without you.

....

Notes

1   This provides an interesting contrast to David's previous experience of the battle front. In their account of the campaign in North Africa, Bierman

and Smith (2002) acknowledge that this 'was a bitter and implacable war in which death came in many terrible ways' (p.1), but they add that this took place 'without hate … virtually without atrocities … Conducted across a largely unpopulated terrain, it provided no scope for the slaughter of non-combatants, intended or inadvertent' (p.2). In 1944, as David moved across Europe, initially in France, then the Netherlands where he was part of Operation Market Garden, and then the invasion of Italy and eventually crossing into Germany itself, his experience of warfare took on a very different dimension. David came to witness what one observer described as 'a new race of troglodytes inhabiting Europe … Thousands upon thousands were living in cellars. Over the piles of rubble to which the towns had been reduced, over the wrecked bridges and blocked waterways, the tangle of twisted metal which had been a railway system, swarmed millions of human beings' (cited in Meehan, 2001, p.31).

2   This was a major airborne attempt to seize control of the Meuse River as well as other canals in order to allow the Allies to gain entry to the Ruhr, Germany's industrial heartland. As previously indicated, the Allied advance was halted; it was indeed, as David described it, 'the sorry affair' and gave Germany some respite.

3   This refers to the regulation that was invoked to intern members of the British Union of Fascists, whose members he had got to know and confront on the streets of the East End in the 1930s. During the war there had already been anger about the relatively benign conditions of their imprisonment, with Sir Oswald Mosley and his wife actually being allowed to share a suite of cells in Brixton Prison. The fact that they were now being released, apparently unrepentant and quickly regrouping, led to a group of Jewish ex-servicemen setting up, in 1945, 'The 43 Group', a clandestine organisation determined to disrupt the fascists physically (see Beckman, 1992).

Five

1945

VICTORY IN EUROPE AND IN
THE GENERAL ELECTION

THIS IS A MOMENTOUS period for it sees what David and Sylvia had predicted for so long: the end of the war. We are still missing Sylvia's letters from this period, as just a few can be found, although more of her voice is heard as David carefully responds to her concerns and queries. Sylvia was both partly still in Frome and back in London, preparing the new home in Walthamstow ready for when David was discharged from the army and they were a family again. She shares many concerns about what that might be like after such a long time apart. David was more optimistic, and was happy with a big change in his circumstances: he was back at base camp acting as camp tailor. He was busy politically, responding with amusement and irritation to news of his family's involvement in the Communist Party and thinking through his own political positions, especially as the 1945 General Election approached and he became the Labour Party's advocate in the ranks. He was also disturbed by what he saw of Germany's suffering and the implications of his being part of the Army of Occupation; he became increasingly involved in the lives of individual Germans, whether the tailors that worked under him or the Jews returning from the camps.

• Wartime Shift of Duties: Regimental Tailor is 'Just What the Doctor Ordered' •

The year 1945 found David with the 2nd Army Group Royal Artillery. David describes their 'crusader' symbol as 'quite a nice sign' (21.02.45), a thick blue cross on a white background with a flaming sword in the centre, all in the shape of a shield. The purpose of the camp was 'keeping the wheels of war going', getting shells to the guns, clothes to the gunners, petrol and spare parts to the vehicles to keep them on the road. It was, David notes, 'one of the best jobs the army offers in terms of safety'. He was well behind the lines, had plenty of creature comforts such as eggs for breakfast and two hot meals a day and the regimental quartermaster called him 'Dave' and even gave him a haircut. He thought he deserved all of this, 'given my record'. He also saw it (30.01 45) as a way of stopping Sylvia from worrying by getting out of the danger he was in while 'on the guns'. All in all, he was now 'feeling my old self again, no pent up nerves, no listening for Jerry's shells, no diving into slit trenches' (12.02.45). He even had time to pick daffodils to put in a vase in his room (12.04.45). It helped that 'I'm an adaptable sort of chap I get by'. His adaptability stretched to the skill of bartering. He asks Sylvia to keep sending him 'cigs' since:

> they come in handy as a form of barter, for eggs, for getting people to do your washing, cigs are worth their weight in gold.

His new and specific role, the camp tailor, was 'all pretty easy' (30.01.45) and 'just what the doctor ordered' (21.02.45), consisting mainly of shortening sleeves and trousers, taking in and letting out, sewing on flashes and stripes, making collars for shorts etc. His sewing machine (21.02.45) was:

> a bit dusty, wanted oiling, I'm getting it fixed up, it will be O.K. I'll soon be accumulating quite a little work-shop.

By March he had as many as six different machines, 'all table top style', but ended up with:

a beauty, the machine folds into a table, oak stands and not iron … a month or two old … I wish I can take it home … still P.G. after the war we shall get one, it's always handy.

Away from work he describes his current billet (21.01.45), which was with a family of two parents and four children, and he made a big fuss of baby Hubert, aged 5 months:

> I've just finished my evening meal, consisting of roast meat and potatoes, peas, rice pudding and coffee, in the best room too, table cloth and all nicely set out, wireless playing.

He was looking forward to sitting 'by the fire in a nice big arm-chair' and then at 10.30 p.m. it was off to 'a real bed room with a bed with an eider down thrown over it'.

As he walked around this quite large front-line town, watching the children playing snowballs, he noticed how the houses were:

> really modern, high ceilings, large rooms, good modern furniture and very clean and they are working class, the standard of living must have been very high, it puts the English way of living in the shade.

There were food shortages, 'money has no value' and many of the men, husbands and sons, had been taken to work in Germany, but everybody looked well dressed and people 'seem to have suffered no undue hardship and that applies to all the countries that I've been through'.

• *News From Home/Preparing For Home* •

He watched those 'lucky chaps' going off on leave and added, 'even if it's not me it's something to look forward to' (28.01.45), and he kept busy making a tie and shirt collars for himself and searching out a new overcoat.

His thoughts frequently turn to his future once discharged, often nudged by the letters from home which kept him entertained, engaged and more. Indeed, all sorts of feelings emerge as he reflects on the political position, especially as he hears of the views being espoused by various family members. News (18.01.45) of his brother-in-law Mick becoming an active communist leaves him 'very much surprised ... wonders will never cease', and he ironically asks whether Mick will leave all his money to 'Joe' (Stalin).

His niece, Gloria, a member of the Young Communist League, wrote to David, but he found her views 'dogmatic' and was impatient with her conviction that 'she going to convert the ordinary worker to communism by shouting Marx or Lenin'. David, in contrast, was determined now to 'concern myself with bread and butter problems'. He accepted that 'the C.P are not the only people to know that the L.P [Labour Party] is not all what it should be', but thought that Gloria should read papers like the *New Leader* and *War Commentary* (an anarchist paper) since their revelations about individual communists would 'make her blood boil'. Nonetheless, David still had a radical streak when it came to 'the Greek position'[1] since:

> I'm afraid I would have found my-self doing what that soldier did refuse to fight, it's a war of intervention pure and simple and a great deal of propaganda of the wrong sort, enough said on that subject one has to be careful of what one writes.

David responds (21.01.45) to concerns that Sylvia had clearly raised about his settling back into home:

> So you've found out a lot of 'ifs' and 'buts' but if I'm willing to bear the responsibilities of Fatherhood with all its worrys, pains anxieties, why should you try and back out of it.

He admits that 'I've not even thought of how I intend making a living after I become demobbed', but he would worry about that 'in all good time', since one thing that he had learnt from the army was 'to live for the day and let the morrow look after it-self'. He was not planning to open a new shop, at least not until his first priority had been met – that holiday with Sylvia and Ruth – and he would work out what to do next 'when I get fed up with being bone idle'.

Subsequently (30.01.45) he considered a political future. In order to pursue this he had to 'brush up on economics if I want to become an M.P' and he included Ruth is his ambitions. She could join him in the Commons as, after all, Lloyd George and his daughter Megan sat together on the parliamentary benches. If he did not make it to MP Sylvia 'might have to be content with being just a Mayoress'.

Sylvia had also, apparently, raised concerns that by the time David returned they would both be 'too old'. David reassures her:

> some chaps have had sexual experiences with women of 15 and they say it was their best ever ... I wouldn't know, but ... you see we've both got along way to go ... I'm not misbehaving, I certainly wouldn't risk V.D. for even Betty Grable.

• Family Business •

The letters from home provided family news, some of it cheering, some worrying, but always with opportunities for comment. He expresses delight at news of Ralph's quick promotion, 'I'm proud of him', and sadness about Evelyn's broken heart, but 'she should consider herself lucky he's gone, only unhappiness would have resulted'. One of Sylvia's sisters, Esther, tells him that another sister, Belle, is very ill and might go into hospital but no one else mentions this, so David wonders if they are trying to protect him or if Esther was exaggerating. He also hears that Millie is worried about Lionel's homecoming, complete with his Canadian bride, and is then glad that 'she turned out to be nice girl' and amused by hearing that Tony told her that she was 'not as nice as your photo.'

David prepared for the future family home through his shopping expeditions, using the army canteen to collect such 'odds and ends' as good lace cloths and dusters, a fretwork model of a Dutch boy and girl in national costume and a notebook from a German school (11.02.45). He worried about the continuing threat of the bombs over London and although he was relieved to hear that their future home, Butterfields, was OK, he says that should it be damaged he would get immediate compassionate leave. In this thinking David was, as Sylvia points out, rather too influenced by all he had seen in Europe, 'homes bombed, looted and pillaged'.

Responding to news of Sylvia's evening at a Red Cross social, he encourages her to get out more (23.01.45) and is enthusiastic about the plans she made for his anticipated leave in February (provided he won the draw) which included a trip to Western-super-Mare and the Cheddar Gorge.

Reassuring Sylvia was not always easy. She was upset when David missed off the customary kisses for her and Ruth; he had to stress (18.02.45) that he did not mean to be 'off hand' and he added an additional sheet with the required big 'X' for each of them. Sylvia's reference to him having a good memory took him back to Betty's wedding:

> the excellence of the bottle of whiskey, where poor little Sylvia <u>nearly</u> lost her virginity, bet that makes you smile.

He worried about money, expressing anger (21.02.45) that the promised Family Allowance was only 5/-. He was 'relieved that I'm going into large-scale robbery so I won't have to rely on this pittance'.

Contrary to this, he was pleasantly surprised (28.01.45) that he had accumulated £149-18-4 in savings, plus other policies: he marks this as a contribution to Ruth's education and this feeds a consistent and pressing emphasis throughout his letters to be involved as a father. He writes (23.01.45) that he is:

> most touched by Ruth's love for me, poor little mite she hardly knows me hope I can live up to the picture of me that you paint for her, if she gets disillusioned it will be your fault.

News of Ruth came from other quarters as well, for example a letter from Aunt (Sylvia's stepmother) which commented on the changes in his daughter: 'she doesn't grumble so much and is really sensible' (18.01.45), and then Gloria redeemed herself with a letter that provided 'snatches of Ruth's playful doings'. He adds that 'Ruth really seems an intelligent child and I'm darn pleased'. He offers some parenting advice (05.02.45) concerning 'that little monkey of mine':

Why not leave her to her fairey dreams, believe me she is living in a glorious land of her own their is plenty of time to disillusion her, but try to explain to her that when she asks you something and please tell her the truth as far as her little mind can take her.

Then he received (15.02.45) the polyphotos of Ruth; his favourite was 'a serious one' and another showed 'a saucy smile, with two mischievous eyes':

I was moved to tears … I just gasped it really took me by surprise, I couldn't imagine that she had grown that fast. She's grand beautiful and intelligent looking, I'm indeed proud of her … when I look at them, then I realise how I miss you both.

• Maintaining his Jewish Identity •

David's Jewish identity was important to him. Earlier (28.09.44) he had described his sadness at missing the service on the eve of the most important Jewish festival, the Day of Atonement:

the first I've missed since I was that high – tho. not a deeply religious man in the orthodox way 'Kol Nedri' always did that little some-thing for me.

Now (15.02.45) there was another Jewish festival pending, the Passover, which is the one perhaps most associated with celebrating around the family table rather than in synagogue. He writes:

You dearest one, will know the answer to 'why is this night different from all other nights' and it's answer, the background of war, death and sorrow will be illiminated by the joy the future will hold not for us alone, but for all the little people, that their struggles shall not be for existence but for the pursuit of happiness, and children will be taught that the last war fought on this Earth was that a government of the people for the people and by the people should not perish from this Earth and that is what I intend fighting for.

He signs off because he has 'to make up a foursome for solo', having won six guilden the last time he played.

He did have (30.03.45) a Seder night, which he 'thoroughly enjoyed' and was held 'under canvass', so not a 'posh affair' but with the customary matzos and wine: 'A lot of the little bits were taken out, but the spirit was there, as well as the wine … we sung all the songs.'

He also met up with Sam (his brother-in-law), who gave a good, solo rendition of *chad gad ya* (a popular song that traditionally ends the service) and later they bunked down together making up a double bed. 'Sam commented that I wasn't obliging like Fay.' David had to leave before the second night but took some matzos and a bottle of wine back for the lads.

David caught up (03.04.45) with news of the family Seder via his niece, Valerie, and he was amused to hear that Ruth had been 'a proper boozer' and that Tony had asked the four questions.

• *On the Frontier of Germany, Stepping In and Out* •

Between the anticipation of Passover in his letter of February and its actual celebration in March, the war had moved on considerably. Returning to that earlier period, David's big news was that 'Your dear husband has actually planted his two feet in Germany' (07.02.45). Although deeply significant, it was a modest advance. He decided to venture 2½ miles to the front line at Sittard where British guns were actually on German soil. This was:

> just to be able to say that I was in Germany, well it was a strange feeling, I was in the German village of Millen, no civilians were their, they had all been evacuated into concentration camps and their homes were left standing with everything in it, well our lads made a mess of the place, beautiful furniture was smashed up for fire wood, sets of crockery were flung against the wall, sewing machines, gramophones were thrown about. Well I'm not going to blame the infantry lads too much, pent up feelings had to have some out-let and there it was, and who was to say no to them, it will be worse the further we go in, what a world!!!

Subsequently (18.02.45) he reassures Sylvia that there was no danger to him when he stepped into Germany:

> papers write such a lot of rot ... each civilian is not an _enemy_, he is jolly glad that it's over for him, that's what I'm told anyway.

Back in Holland David had a new billet:

> a farm house miles from anywhere and sleeping in a hay loft, its not as it sounds, we have the run of the house during the day. It's a proper farm, smells like one too, cows, chickens, pigs and horses, we have plenty of fresh milk and an egg every day and whats more real pre war Dutch cheese, I'm getting as fat as the little pigs themselves. The family consists of Mother and Father in the late thirties. 4 children all boys, ages ranging from 7 to 2 years of age and the Mother about 8 months gone and only been married just over ten years not bad going eh? I find this all over Holland, North and South they marry late in life the girl always over 25 and nearer 30 and then men between 30 and 40 and then they commence family life in earnest, where-ever you go, women seem to be in a perpetual state of [illegible] their time – just had it – just beginning ... one thing stands out the men look well, the women weary.

If the birth happened while David and his unit were still around there would be:

> duties aloted to us, I don't think there is any Doctor about. Paddy a driver gets our M.O. Joe who is a butcher cuts the naval cord, our Sgt Major will slap it on the back and the rest will get the hot water going, we are all hoping it will come out at a reasonable hour of the day.

Indeed, when a baby girl was born, at 4.30 in the morning, David witnessed the birth:

> it came out with pain and had blood on its body   perhaps this world is being born again, this period may be its 'pain' and blood, lets see that we wash it clean when peace comes, lets leave no bad blood, no dirt, no germs for in these things lie this evil thing men call war.

David went on (18.02.45) to express his concern about the big three conferences being prepared for the political leaders of the Allied forces, but 'I shall pass no judgement … until the full proposals are published'.

David became involved with civilians in the area. An example he gives (12.02.45) is of a man coming to his billet and telling how he and his family had escaped from a German-held town and that he had a sister married to an Englishman living in Preston. David offered, because there was no civilian post as yet, to write and reassure the Preston family and he subsequently received a letter (05.02.45) from a Gerard Turner, who wrote:

> I cannot express in words how grateful I am to hear that my wife's family is safe. For months now we have both been worried beyond endurance as to what might have happened to them … If you could see my wife now you would be more than gratified. May God bless you for your kindness, and may he keep you safe and guide you back to those whom you love.

On the move again (21.02.45), the family presented him with a large cake and thirty eggs,: 'the Dutch are grand people.' Now he was in:

> a deserted village, no people, no gas, no electric and the drainage system smells, beautiful homes and furniture wrecked and smashed it's a rotten shame.

Nonetheless they had found one house that was in good condition and they 'made ourselves very comfortable'. There was an electric washing machine with a mangle attached, along with 'some good drying weather', so he could 'get cracking on our washing'. Despite all this, he felt sad when he saw the scattered children's toys and family pictures on the wall.

The hospitality of the local people is further evidenced when, on a trip to Brussels to get supplies, he had to stay overnight:

> So we stopped in a town and knocked on a likely looking house to put the two of us up, well they did it with pleasure, not only that they let us have cooking utensils for our late dinner and then at supper time we had two fried eggs apiece (they kept chickens) and in the morning she had boiled an egg for our journey … that is not unusual.

• David in Germany: 'Pay Off Time' •

By February (28.02.45) he was back in Germany, and this time not just for a quick visit to the border. He was now in 'what was a rather large sized German town', which he later identifies as Kleve, but 'there's not a house standing' so their quarters were the cellars of the homes, 'fine big underground rooms' which had previously been used by civilians. The cellars had 'been partitioned off and in our particular one, was a kitchen and a bedroom'. The kitchen had a stove, table, chairs, plates and cutlery and the bedroom had bedding. There were books, children's toys again and family albums from which he took some photos to send home to Sylvia. He comments that these were taken between 1940 and 1942 and that 'they don't look very starving'. There was also a copy of *Mein Kampf*, presented to a couple on the occasion of a wedding. Although the houses seemed to have been in good condition and well equipped with everything that makes 'a decent home', all this was smashed up:

> the boys are leaving nothing for Jerry to come home to ... I dont like it, its not civilisation but I can justify it ... this is the pay off.

David describes some of the German radio propaganda, citing 'Mary of Arnhem', which was:

> clever ... You'll hear the chimes of Big Ben and the very English voice telling you that it is Joseph MacCloud speaking and then she comes in, perfect timing, she gives her news, and then cheekily says 'this is the end of the news and I shall switch you back to the B.B.C. thank you for listening'. There is another programme, 'Jerry Calling' that cuts out B.L.A.2 and plays 'Home Sweet Home' every five minutes. It will go something like this 'are you knee deep in mud? is your slit trench full of water? and other such discomforts' and then finishes off mournfully playing 'Home Sweet Home.' Another tactic is when an American programme ends with the words DON'T FRATERNISE and Jerry cuts in with a witty song, sung sneeringly about non fraternisation. I'm writing this for interest and to show that Jerry is certainly clever.

David also sent Sylvia, 'just out of interest', various army news-sheets, including his unit's *The Corps Courier*.

Being in Germany clearly influenced David's picture of the war; it seemed to be:

> going great guns … all day and night tanks rumble thro. the streets, guns flash and thunder in the distance and our aircraft are over every hour of the day

However, the actual victory still eluded them:

> Blast the German people why don't they have the spunk to kick Hitler out, than be like sheep led to the slaughter. A nation like that deserves all it gets, the prisoners we see along the road typify a people who don't care if they live or die, it's a sorry sight, for the German people have had greatness.

Then his mood shifts. Pushing on through Germany, and looking forward to crossing the Rhine, he observes (07.03.45):

> how even isolated houses and buildings are bashed about … Plenty of German people are seen trying to salvage out of ruins what was left of their home. After five years of war I can still find compassion in my heart. In this suffering world, if we still hate I see no hope for the future.

He was also hurt and angered by the losses of his own side. This was in response to Sylvia's reference to a Mrs Smith, a widow (07.03.45):

> There are a lot of Mrs Smiths about and many a time in the past you were nearly one of them, it's a bloody shame, I will never get used to this death and desolation, sorrow that can only be stilled but never hushed, love and memories of a dead love that keeps your mind alive but your body dead, its to the living that it matters, he's dead, he feels nothing: he's not even a MO., nobody wants the job of burying him, he lies with a blanket over him and his feet sticking out, he is not mortal any-more, and I am beginning to wonder whether he even becomes immortal, death we see out here is not beautiful, it ugly, it smells, cut short, and we call them 'stiffs' – I'm bitter,

I've seen some of my best friends like that – that's war. Now I'm sorry I'm writing in this strain, but its good to get it off my chest and I know you don't want me ever to kid you.

A period of leave, in Louvain, brought some relief to all of this pressure (16.03.45). The place he stayed in was nice, with good food, but it was quiet compared to Brussels and it was hard to buy gifts as they were either too expensive, 'silk stockings are 275 francs', or not very good quality. He got a birthday card for Ruth and skittles. What he would really have liked to get home were the sewing machines, but they were classified as 'loot'; however, he kept hold of the copy of *Mein Kampf*. For entertainment he went to the pictures and:

> to-night is a dance, 50 local A.T.S. girls are invited, so a good time should be had by all, but don't worry about me, it's lucky I cant dance.

Billeted (18.03.45) with a German family, he muses on how 'very hard' it was:

> not to fraternise, they give us eggs and milk, they have two nice girls aged seven and ten. We try hard to be indiferent, but you cant turn aside good deeds, with out a thank you.[2]

He was proud that his knowledge of Yiddish allowed him to be used as an interpreter.

A few days later (25.03.45):

> amidst glorious sunshine and a very clear sky I saw those air-borne and paratroop divisions pass over what a sight the sky was darkened for half an hour … they seemed invincible and they were and so the great assault on the Rhine was made and its doing very well, how long now? not long it can't be.

Alongside this he was trying to make sense of the Germans he saw; he was impressed (13.04.45) at the way that 'men raise their hats to women and they shake hands, it seems they have civilised customs'.

Then one 'lovely' Sunday (25.03.45):

> all our <u>German friends</u> are dressed up to kill and are off to Church, what
> they pray for I don't know, their family life is very similar to civilised
> people, friends come to visit them and stay for coffee, young girls go for a
> stroll, children play games in the fields, I can detect nothing barbaric in the
> behaviour of these people. I certainly think that there is hope for them yet,
> about 25 years tuition and they will learn the democratic way of life.

He responds to some concerns from Sylvia (31.03.45) and assures her
that:

> there's more good than bad, I, even with all the cries and suffering of our
> German Jews and others in my minds eye, can not find hate in my heart,
> not for these country folk any-way. People that till the land and sow the
> fruits of the earth and make that land fertile, have little say in the system of
> their governments, they who I hate are the leaders.

Meanwhile, the war was moving on rapidly (31.03.45), too fast, in fact, for
his regiment's 'lumbering big guns, tanks will be just the job for finishing
off this last phase of the war'. Being out of the immediate war zone, 'out
of the line', gave him time to reflect on his war years, the series of battles
of rivers and canals, the Seine, the Marne, the Leopold Canal, the Mars,
the Leck, the Roer and now the Rhine: 'I've been across the whole darn
shot of them.'

In April (03.04.45) he reported being 'very busy', which was 'keeping
me out of trouble'. The 'weather is lousy' but he was in:

> a jolly good billet, an empty German house and in very good condition
> and well stocked with preserved goods, like peas, carotts, coli-flower, small
> cucumbers, and of all things pickled wall-nuts, naturally they are filling our
> tummy's now and its just the job.

What he did not enjoy, though, was being part of the Army of Occupation
(13.04.45). There were:

too many children and old people that you've got to be firm, it'll get under our skins before long. Remember Steinbeck's 'the Moon is down' well it'll be very much the same thing, I'm hoping that it wont last long, and that we shift about and not stay too long in one place, I'm a sentimental old soul, I wish I can be hard hearted.

This led to his thoughts (13.05.45) about the non-fraternisation rule:

it means fighting old men, women and children with the same weapon that the German then released on other countries, it wont ensure peace.

• *Family News and all its Complications* •

During this period David continued to comment on family matters, much of it focused on Lionel, which is understandable since it could have meant that Millie, the eldest of Sylvia's sisters and mainstay of the family, could move to Canada with Lionel, who hoped for a post-war career in civil aviation there. David thought he would be best back in England. He imagines (13.03.45) that Lionel will have:

changed quite a bit, the thought that one can command and be obeyed puts a different complex on ones life, its for better or for worse, hope its for better and not the other, I've seen too much of the other.

Then (20.03.45), responding to apparent concerns that Bea, Lionel's fiancée, would not be living on £30 a week, as she had anticipated, but rather £8, he says 'my heart bleeds for her' and this returns him to the theme of officers who were, for the most part, 'highly over-paid' and tended to be 'big headed'. A 'bad one [officer] is truly a bastard, a good one worth his weight in gold'. In the letter he apologises if he shocked her with such language, but 'it's the Kings English'.

David hears that Lionel is offering to take Alf on as one of his ground crew, but is not certain that the move would be a good one for his brother, and worries (01.04.45) about not having heard from Alf for months. David wonders if:

he might be best off going to Canada and marry a girl friend of Bea's for if he stays in England and does not settle down, he'll be a continual source of worry to Mother.

Even hearing from Alf (15.04.45) provides little comfort; he thinks that he:

hides his real thoughts behind a mask of jokes and cheap talk ... I feel so far away from him ... he is as you say very unsettled, he must find himself again, feel sure I could talk to him.

This turns David to a general comment about contemporary life (01.04.45) and he declares that he is:

not worried who he marries, as long as he is happy and that applies to Jew or gentile, these days a man must lead his own life according to his own convictions and not custom or religion. Honestly I shan't demand any thing of my children that is any thing obligatory, my attitude will not be that I am your <u>father</u>, but more of a good pal or friend.

Returning (04.03.45) to his daughter, he is so 'pleased' with:

the progress Ruth is making, she sounds bright, still its to be expected, it will soon be her fifth birthday we'll see what she makes of school, not much I think, not at first, she wont like the discipline the teacher will <u>try</u> to impose.

When he gets a detailed story of that first day at school (25.04.45) he is both pleased and amused:

the picking of flowers for teacher, the regret at having Saturday and Sunday off ... she must be keen, bless her heart I can really picture her taking her partners hands and walking into school, I bet she looks fine ... Re Ruth's saying of prayers, well don't let it worry you, she'll know soon enough what Jewishness implies and understand her position, now it doesn't really matter, but should she ask questions try and answer them, the way they should be answered.

He had been able to find some gifts for her (18.03.45) of 'a <u>very, very nice</u> box of picture blocks and also a two tier pencil box in readiness of school'.

He also had gifts for the other children: for Tony there was a game of skittles and the same pencil box, and for Jeffery 'a kind of wood Meccano set, it cost a bob or two'. He got Sylvia something for the home but kept this 'under his hat', admitting only that it was pretty.

• *David's Relationship with Sylvia: 'No Morals [But] a Hell of a Lot of Scrupples'* •

Concerning David's relationship with Sylvia, this was a frustrating period. In one letter (25.03.45) he appreciates that:

> this lonliness is more for you than it is for me, I have the excitment of events that kind of take away that ache for you a little, a very little little, but it helps, those empty months of yours must be real and truly empty.

He shares (18.03.45) a story with her, an episode in Belgium when:

> I was approached … by a young woman dressed in black, not pretty but not plain and able to ask in good but halting English whether I was carrying some thing for sexual intercourse? because, if so, you can use it with me.

David was taken aback but asked how much, and she explained 'it was not commercial'. She explained that her man had been sent to Germany several years earlier and 'he had taught her how to love and she now found it difficult to live with out it'.

David agreed to meet her the next evening, with her asking him to bring 'more than one you'll find me a difficult woman', but he was ten minutes late and saw her going off with another soldier, 'which really amused me, any body does'. He adds:

> so you see dearest what pit falls there are for us lonely soldiers, its lucky for you that tho I have no morals, I have a hell of a lot of scruples and that makes a big difference.

There is no direct record of Sylvia's response to this but clearly she did comment because he returns (31.03.45) to the 'woman in black' incident and his 'honest answer' is that he had only one contraceptive on him, and this he had to 'borow off one of the chaps, I don't usually carry them about with me'. He admits:

> I might have gone with her, I don't know, but fate played her part well and I was glad, this is not the first occasion when I might have had and didn't … scrupples bade otherwise.

He also tells Sylvia not to have too much sympathy for the woman, 'she has a novel and original line, but that she is a prostitute I have no dought'.

When Sylvia makes a reference to VD, he reassures her (11.04.45) that the risks are exaggerated, as it 'is only dangerous when neglected' and adds, 'believe me nobody feels a man until he has had a "dose"'. He asks Sylvia not to get 'hot under the collar about it'. He will soon be home and away from all temptation so 'now we'll leave the subject in the gutter where it belongs'.[3]

With the chance of leave in Brussels he is reminded (13.04.45) of previous periods in the city and he is determined not to visit any:

> low dives this time, I've seen all the gutter life I want from the smelly East, to the more modern vice clubs of the continent, this barter of bodies is an international cartel, spreading its dirty claws right thro. the world – poverty and war is its breeding ground.

Alongside this rather stark and matter-of-fact approach to sex there is a letter (03.04.45), intended to reach Sylvia by their wedding anniversary (on the 8th of that month), where he reflects how:

> You know what that means to both of us, it was to us as if the Lord blessed that day and made it Holy, and as in the beginning of creation he looked opon the finished Earth and said it was good, so on that day he must have uttered those words again, for our marriage dearest mine, was surely made in heaven, and in order to test it, he gave us the temptations of Adam and Eve, the sufferings of Job but he also gave us faith of Moses and the wisdom

of Soloman and that's why our love has been so great ... our marriage thro' partings and pain has stood the test of time and for <u>all time</u>. Thanks sweetheart mine for giving me every thing to come back too, you've been a beacon if light thru. these long – long months of parting, my hopes for the future are that with Gods help that soon I'll be with you and to spend our lives in peace and happiness.

Sylvia's description of Ruth's birthday party leaves him feeling 'so proud' (08.04.45) of being the father of a 5-year-old. He recalls her birth: although weighing less than 6lb 'she was a little being'. David is pleased that she is drinking her milk without any trouble:

you know dearest my thoughts are completely of her these last few days – I'm getting home sick how I miss you both.

He is proud of Sylvia, especially how:

you stood every thing that Jerry slung over just to keep the shop going, and you never complained, your letters always showed courage and you've brought up Ruth with inteligence and understanding, and what is most important of all is that you gave me hope and faith to bear my part with the same courage.

He goes on to worry about how she will manage getting back to London; she would have 'a hell of a lot of things to carry' and he was not helping with the bits and pieces he was sending her. The latest present from the 'Third Reich' was a biscuit barrel that he thought was pretty and was intended as 'a little compensation for being bombed'. He had also a 1945 diary complete with swastika and a portrait of 'that man'. He was pleased that it would be 'the last diary ever to be printed in Natzi Germany':

I've not been near a gun since Dec 1st, no more digging gun pits, firing barrages, standing too in rain, snow and muck, no more night firing, fearing not the strange sounds of night, sleeping with my trousers on and not wondering whether I'll be disturbed by the sounds of shells bursting, or the continual hell noise of our big guns, what a change, how I appreciate it, still it did not come too soon, if I'd stayed much longer in that Nigmeyan area I'm sure I would have broken down, I nearly reached breaking point when we were shelled out of two positions in one day and lost three killed and six wounded. Now I can watch the flowers beginning to bloom the trees in full bud, Spring is well on the way and all the while destruction is sweeping the world.

The next day (09.04.45) found him still very full of memories following a letter from Sylvia that did survive, marking their wedding anniversary:

April 8th 1945

Darling husband of mine,

This is the anniversary of our wedding night, &, alone, I can't celebrate the occasion in the correct manner. And surely, that event does deserve being recalled – tonight of all nights. Please God, in a short while now, I know we shall re-live that night – re-live it every single night of your leave – making of your week another grand honeymoon. Bless, dearest Dave, I love you very much …

Your letter (which arrived yesterday) was beautifully worded, and your references to the Bible were appreciated – our marriage was indeed made in Heaven, and I have for a husband the dearest angel of them all.

So you are interested in the negligee I referred to – I will certainly get one at the first opportunity as you imply that I can afford such a luxury.

What follows are various comments about the wider family, including some digs at Bea, who had 'exactly 22 pairs' of silk stockings and who did not write letters either to David or Millie:

On the frequent occasions when she complained of feeling bored, it would have done her no harm to settle down to answering her correspondence … This, to me, shows a lack of respect on her part – ignorance as you term it.

Then back to David's leave: 'I would like my full seven nights with you, darling mine – I don't want to forego a single one.'

David (09.04.45) had spent the anniversary on watch 'so thro the lonely watch my mind was full of memories and my heart full of fond reflections'.

He notes Sylvia's comment that they had spent more of their married life apart than together, and she seemed worried about her 'little faults'. David simply replies that:

> I've had to put up with such a lot of petty and silly things in the army, that what you call faults will be the highest of virtues.

He had been listening to 'the Count of Monti Cristo' on the radio and that reminds him of how 'we used to plan our radio program, such a lot of nice things we used to do, and so much _nicer_ things'.

His family connections were reinforced (13.04.45) when he received a birthday card from Sylvia and Ruth, and although he was sad that this was his only card, 'folks must have missed it'. Nonetheless, he reports that although 33, he 'feels 10 years younger' and is 'fit and well'.

Another letter of Sylvia's (19.04.45) has her responding to various presents from David, a paper rack for Tony and Ruth, pencils and some stamps for another niece, Valerie, who was 'very thrilled with them … (no wonder you are her favourite uncle)'. In return she looked for a birthday present for David, 'everywhere for something … without any luck', until she came across:

> a really beautiful chromium frame for your photo – an expensive one, and one I wouldn't normally have considered.

She was then (01.06.45) surprised to receive from David:

> a tremendous bouquet brought – by hand – delivered through the leading local florist … I don't think I've ever seen such a lovely collection … a mix of huge pink flowers … delicate-looking mauve flowers … Sweet Williams – two colours – a large bunch of pinks … and a few sprays of gyp. I feel proud being the object of so much love and esteem.

To add emphasis she wrote this on 'special notepaper for a rather special letter' and she also commented on the more ordinary matters of wartime Britain: namely the expense of getting her watch fixed, £6-10-0, a startling contrast to the £2-10-0 she paid for it when she bought it nine and a half years earlier.

• *Leave in Brussels* •

When he got to Brussels David found (17.04.45) that where previously he had stayed in a posh hotel he was now billeted with a childless, middle-aged couple. As he sat drinking ice-cold beer and eating ice cream he was struck by how distant the war seemed, 'nobody seems to work and every day looks like a Saturday afternoon'. He missed Sylvia as he watched couples go by, walking arm in arm, and he imagined her:

> by my side, wearing a nice flowered summery frock and beautiful even in the heat of the day and wearing your sun glasses, making you look even more seductive than ever.

He felt lonely, also, because he did not team up with anyone, not finding any of his fellow soldiers being 'the types I like', but he quickly met up with French, Belgium, Polish and American soldiers, as well as many civilians, which allowed him to get 'some more material on my experiences of life'. A couple of days later (19.04.45) he enjoyed 'the pulse of life in the hustle and bustle of a metropolis', but prices had shot up. He went to a funfair and happened across a shooting range where if you hit the bull's eye, Hitler's heart, it lit up. He got six shots for 20 francs and hit the target twice, 'not bad eh!?'

His work shifted (23.04.45) as he took on interpreting for German-speaking Russian, Polish and Italian slave workers, although he says very little about this beyond a later comment (02.05.45) that:

> Germany seems full of them, all roaming the country waiting to be picked up, full of smiles and some times up to no good, they are apt to take things on the robbing and violence style, I suppose you can't blame them.[4]

Although he heard a great deal about the impact of the Nazi war machine, this did not stop him from wanting to know more about the German civilians he saw on the streets; indeed, it left him even more curious:

> I would like to … find out what they are thinking and saying its so difficult to feel their pulse.

He talks about being in:

> a nice part of Germany, the town is pretty … there's still running water and electric light, the place is hardly touched, the war passed by its way very quickly. [Of the people] their lives are restricted, a curfew exists, we take what ever militorily we want, if necessary turn them out of their houses, but for all that we are pretty just but firm, I don't think we ever abuse our authority. Life is very much the same here as in any other small town, farming goes on as usual, there is not a lot work to be done other than farming … There are no young men about, but plenty of young girls, they go strolling in the evening trying to be most pleasant to the soldiers, like Tommy's are finding it really hard to non fraternise, for they are really well built and pretty looking, well dressed too, I suppose love will find way.

He notes the shocking extent of the bomb damage, 'but it seems that was the only way to bring Germany to its knees and they started it' (01.06.45).

• *At Last, Leave Home … and Victory in Europe* •

David (28.04.45) got excited with the promise of forthcoming leave, planned for 9 May, but he did not know whether Sylvia was back in London; indeed, he was so unsure that he first put the Frome address on the envelope, before crossing it out and replacing it with 'Butterfields'. He gave the time he was due at Victoria but advised her also to phone the station in advance to confirm whether he was, in fact, arriving on that day or the day before or after. If Sylvia was not there to meet him he would ring the family in Frome or put a trunk call to the fishmongers. It was, as he admits, all very complicated, which he put down to his being 'a bit too excited to work it all clearly ... I just feel too much for words'. The confusion is understandable as getting back entailed a 'hell of a journey' (02.05.45), taking all of three days to get from the regiment to home. He was full of plans: helping to sort the house, getting the gas laid on etc. Sylvia raised a question about the 'horror camps', news of which was just emerging to the wider public, but David wanted to delay his own responses to when they met: 'I can talk better than I can write I feel very strongly on a lot of things.' He ends:

> So cheers darling mine, God Bless you and Ruth, shall be seeing you soon Always yours David X for you X for Ruth.

The excitement was then increased (04.05.45) by the latest war news, which came through even as he was writing his letter:

> German soldiers in the whole Western Germany and Denmark have give in – well its all over, I always thought I shall be home in a peaceful England and my hopes have come true ... it's been tough for every body but it's over, now perhaps we can look forward with hope and confidence to the peaceful years ahead <u>together</u>.

The prospect of being home for Victory Week was 'grand'.

• *Back From Leave, and 'It's Stormy Weather'* •

The impact of the leave home stayed with David for some time. A 'short and hurried note' (23.05.45) starts with the words of the song *Stormy Weather*, 'I don't know why there's no sun up in the sky, stormy weather', which summed up his life just then:

> as the rain beats down, so I can feel the beating of the drums, the strings of the violin and the blaring out of the saxophone as it moans out, 'Can't go on, every thing I have is gone, stormy weather, keeps raining all the time'.

He hoped to 'snap out' of this mood soon and be back 'to my usual self', but he was still relishing the time they had spent together; how he had experienced 'your great love, your steadfastness in virtue and your courage in parting' which allowed him to anticipate leaving the war behind and a future 'with all its happiness and love'. He returned to the theme the next day (24.05.45), musing on the '11 days and nights', which were like a:

> wonderful dream … a love story in the films … The joys we taste are so much sweeter for we know it lasts for just so long, we take our love in great gulps, breathing in its exotic excitement and dispelling it with the greatest of reluctance, that is why parting comes with tears and sorrow … and there is a 'morrow' and that day will dispel all tears, fears and sorrow.

Indeed, the 'morrow' could be quite soon: 'according to the news back at camp' he could be discharged by Christmas or shortly afterwards, and he also got confirmation that he would not be called upon for future active service.

For Sylvia too the leave was important, as one of the letters that survive from this period makes clear:

20.05.1945, 9.45

Dearly beloved.

It is only a little over half an hour since we said goodbye, but I felt I wanted to write to you now – just to reassure you that everything is O.K.

I'm honestly sorry I let myself get so upset – the tears were there and I couldn't keep them bottled up any longer. After we had left you, though, I seemed to feel a lot easier and almost happier – It was the waiting that was so hard to bear – watching the clock and realising that our precious hours together were fast slipping away. Now that you have gone, the first pain of parting seems to have gone too – I have left sweet thoughts of the memory of a grand long leave. Our every moment was filled with happiness – the joy of being together again. Soon now – <u>very</u> soon, I feel sure – we shall see an end of all these trials – God bless you, David, I love you so very much.

Bon voyage my darling husband – and may God speed you back home
to us.

Always my deepest devotion,

Yours alone,

Sylvia.

X from me
X from Ruth

PS. Looking through the desk, I have just come across your Board of Trade
forms. They are the same, exactly, as the one I sent in, so you needn't bother
about registering.
God bless – Sylvia.

• *Hamburg: 'Should Be Interesting'* *and More News of Life as a Soldier* •

David knew (24.05.45) that his next location would be Hamburg, which,
with its entertainments, swimming and boating, 'should be interesting'.

His next letter (25.05.45) gives the details: he was staying in a suburb,
which must have once been fine, but 'the R.A.F. sent down beautiful
bombs and made it ugly'. By his estimate 75 per cent of the area had been
badly bombed and his own billet was 'parcially damaged and blasted',
which were the same conditions for the local people who were still
living there.[5]

Despite this devastation, David noticed children playing and young
girls sunbathing, but he was angry with the non-fraternisation policy, not
just because it stopped him from talking to these women, but because:

thro. speech there is hope, silence only breeds misunderstanding and
mistrust. hope this hatred abates and we give Germany a chance to play its
part in the prosperity of the world.

He describes (27.05.45) tram cars:

carrying people some place some where. The army has commodeared all places of amusements like cinemas, theatres and Hotels. Hotels have become super NAAFI's, Y.M.C.AS and such like, complete with band (German) the food in these places just consist of tea and cake and that's all. There's an open air pool, very nice and comfortable, large too and they have certain hours they can go and their part of the pool is roped off … it's all very agravating and tantalising to see young healthy bodies dressed in the latest and scantiest bathing costumes, behind a rope with big letters stating VERBOTEN … the young lads are biting nails and generally fed up.

A later letter (04.06.45) describes the Elbe River as:

a grand and imposing swift flowing river, its embankments twist thro parklands and wooded [illegible] with stately trees, truly a place where love can only be spoken and its beauty felt. I feel sure I desicrate its path with my hobnailed boots.

This acts as a further contrast to the:

grand Hotels and beautiful houses that are there no more. It all seems so tragic that one man was allowed to create such havoc.

David promises that this is another of the places that they will visit together one day. For the most part he got on with the life of a soldier. This could involve big events like (02.06.45) a:

great 'do', a thanksgiving service, a march past and all the trimmings of a military ceremony it was impressive and I enjoyed it.

There was (05.06.45) the excited anticipation of the men at the arrival of the ATS, although it would be tough with 2,000 men for each girl:

but I think the lads would prefer the 'frenchies' it's what they wear that attracts. Flowered frocks, light coloured dresses, showing off fine limbs and busts, where-as the A.T.S. with their serge Khaki uniform, thick stockings, puts the lads off ... In Belgium and Holland where there were pretty girls we took them for granted, but here in Germany the lads are finding beauty in any thing that wears skirts, it's all so silly, especially when we know how the Russians are acting quite differently.

As for the rest of his time, he enjoyed the 'grand' weather and the 'plenty of swimming'. At times he fretted over his German (05.06.45), which was not improving, and he kept mixing it up with Yiddish. Neither was he getting letters (29.05.45), either from Sylvia or any other family members, but he put this down to being 'just unlucky' with the deliveries. For the most part, however, he got on with his work and was pleased that his 'reputation' as a tailor had made him 'quite an important personage', as he went 'down to the battery's [to] fit the lads up, conflab with Majors and other lesser beings as to what wanted altering'.

He had 'a brisk trade' and it changed his relationship with the officers: 'the little Hitlers with stripes' were more like 'sugar daddies than bold bad villains' since they all came to David for smartening up (21.06.45).

He was also busy (17.06.45) with various educational schemes, which included social history, economics and citizenship, and his cultural life was enriched (21.06.45) by visits from the Old Vic Theatre Company and their productions of Ibsen's *Peer Gynt* with Laurence Olivier and Ralph Richardson. David went twice, the better to understand it, and he enjoyed the experience enormously – 'you know how much I like Grieg's music' – while Richardson's performance was:

> a terrific piece of acting, he commands the stage like a thief, robs you of your character and gives you Peer Gynt's ... a grand play and a grand cast.

He was also (24.06.45) looking forward to a rather different entertainment, 'a tip top circus with all the fun of the fair' and the promise of:

> a famous strip tease artist and her troup of girls out of uniform, promises to be sensous and sensational, so I should be well amused.

He was (19.06.45) happy with his appearance. Following a heat wave he was:

quite my Middle East self brownish looking, it's improving my looks honest Sylvia dear I feel as fit as a fiddle, I'm sure that my army life apart from its hardships has toughened me and taken at least ten years off my age in health and everything.

• *David's Mind is on Home and the War: 'It all Seems so Long Ago'* •

For all this, his mind was very much on what was happening back home. His next letter (31.05.45), by which time he had received two from Sylvia, shows just how much he was feeling himself into home again. He relishes the images of the Sabbath candles being lit on a Friday night and the cat asleep on Sylvia's lap. He fusses over Ruth's education and whether 'the active school stuff', although it sounds progressive, gets results, and about the standards for scholarships. He is not too worried however: 'brains will out in any kind of education system'. He is impressed by Ruth's success in a race and actually prints out in block letters at the end:

DADDY IS GLAD YOU CAME SECOND IN THE RACE AT THE PARTY. YOU'RE A GOOD GIRL AND I SEND YOU A BIG KISS. GOD BLESS, DADDY.

A letter from Gloria reinforces (05.06.45) his picture of Ruth's cleverness and skills at drawing; clearly she was:

real observant and what is more important it shows reasoning quite beyond her years, that's Gloria's opinion too … I'm expecting big things P.G. in the years to come.

He thanks God for his safety and the chance to see his children grow up. He pictures Sylvia entering the life of Butterfields and getting involved in that neighbourhood, and anticipates how much of a help that will be when he starts his political career. He is (05.06.45) shocked by what he hears of life back in Britain, especially prices; for example the cost of a watch repair:

The price that was needed ... some-what shook me, but why worry, thats why I left you that money to spend how you like.

David collected all sorts of things that would be 'handy' when he returned:

> yds and yds of calico or some linen material, well at least 10yds and very wide, make good curtaining material and also some silken or some such material petticoats but no knickers.

He would hang on to them until his next leave, otherwise 'there may be trouble'.

The anniversary of D-Day (07.06.45) reminds him of all that he has been through and how 'it seems a long time ago'. He lists:

> the Arrarmanches beach head, Bayeux, Argentian, Falaeiil, the Seine, events that was hucked with hard punches and a hell of a lot of thrills. I showed in most of them and in that I was proud.

This was not just a looking back, however; he was invoking the fighting spirit, 'the boldness of these adventures', in the hope that it could be 'carried through in a brave new world heralded in by voting Labour'. The forthcoming General Election was increasingly on his mind and he wondered whether Sylvia would be talked into working for the Labour Party, although 'I'll be amazed if you do'. Nonetheless, he was anxious (09.06.45) for news of the election and wanted copies of the party manifestos and reports from meetings of the candidates:

> give me your reflections, see what you think, this keep me in touch with the great happening at home.

Not all that was 'happening at home' was very satisfactory: there is a letter from one sister-in-law which is lengthy but 'all trouble as usual'; another sister-in-law complains about not having heard from Sylvia. 'She is searching her conscience and finds it quite clear' and although he asks Sylvia to 'try and rectify this', he adds, defensively perhaps, 'not that I care' (12.06.45). Within a day a letter from Sylvia puts him in a better mood and (13.06.45) provides 'a nice bit of homely news', including his daughter's art work, done with:

> such intelligence and reasons why and when that I'm beginning to think that perhaps we have a daughter that will grow beautiful in mind and body … I can just picture you all so vividly that it almost hurts.

He anticipated being home by August and September, and having 'a chest full' of medals, four in all, the Africa star, Italy star, France and Germany and the 1939–45 star.

He describes the weather, rain and thunder storms, 'not like June at all', and while he has eaten some strawberries, they are 'a bit sour … I had no cream to go with them', which represents, perhaps, his feelings about Germany overall.

• The General Election is Pending and 'Naturally' David is 'Chief Labour Spokesman' •

David kept an ear to the wider, political world. As far as the war was concerned (26.06.45) his old friend and comrade, Phil, writes from Damascus and is very bitter against the French; David adds: 'and our attitude was right and correct.' David's growing preoccupation (30.06.45) with the forthcoming General Election was partly practical; he needed to get his name on the electoral roll and he was busy reading all the press he could get hold of: the *Express*, *Mail*, *Herald* and *Mirror*.

In the same letter he has to address other more immediate problems, such as a letter to the building society and checking when the Jewish New Year will be, followed by an exclamation:

> My! What you two grown up children talk about, divorce and such nonsense, I liked that bit about the custody of <u>our children</u> well if we are going to have more than one, it implies that I'll be living on very intimate terms with you for a long time (PG) so why worry … seeing that I'll never attain that position where I'll be able to afford a divorce your pretty safe with me for the next hundred years.

Other letters chart the gathering pace of the election. David enjoys (05.07.45) Sylvia's account of an election meeting which was addressed by prominent Labour politicians, both of whom David had heard speak before, and he was glad that 'you are on waving terms with future MPs'. Just getting the news (30.06.45):

> makes me feel that world reading events are part of you too, I enjoy the thrill of being part and parcel of moving and stirring times.

The 'election fever' was strong in his camp and:

> naturally I'm chief Labour spokesman in any of the arguments at the dinner table and canteen. We have some good fun, needless to say 90% are Labour … I shall be eagerly awaiting the results, here's hoping for good Labour victory, it does mean a lot to all of us. Ruth, I'm afraid will grow up (that is if I decide to do things politically) in a political atmosphere. I think it will do her no harm. I'd like her to look back in her youth and say that she knew real people.

David (11.07.45) was 'darn pleased' that Sylvia had recorded his vote, as pleased as he was cross with Fay voting, as her husband Sam directed her to, for the Liberals – this was 'a shocking waste of a vote'.

Meanwhile, he was on the move again (09.07.45), to Essen, which may have been 250 miles nearer to home, but still felt a long way away. It was 'a grand trip' down the Autobahns, which were 'wonderful roads' and gave David a chance to see more of Germany, a 'beautiful country' with little obvious damage until they reached the Ruhr: 'well, it was just terrible.' His billet was in Bochum, 'a lovely place, not so countryfed, more like Ilford', which provokes in David the now familiar feeling of sadness at the contrast between what might have been and what Hitler brought:

> Its such a pity that Germany went the way she did, she has nice towns, a standard of living and the people look homely and intelligent, its a pity, she should and could be great, perhaps in the future she will, in a democratic way.

He was now living in a modern block of working-class flats, with a nice tiled bathroom and central heating with a lot of the original furniture:

> these people could certainly show us something about living and building ... we live like lords and as usual at some peoples expense, we probably put women and children out, just to show we are top dog.

After writing his letter he planned to take a walk; it as a nice evening and 'non frat' had been lifted so he could now 'get to see what the local "talent" is like and keep an eye open for a nice young girl'. He adds that Sylvia can tell any women at home, worried by the news of the lifting of the ban, that:

> in Belguim and Holland where verginity was bought for just one bar of choc or a packet of cigs, most men were faithful to their wives at home.

He had to revise this statement quite quickly; he is 'disgusted' (13.07.45) with:

> Tommics and fraulines now walking openly hand in hand ... and not just holding hands, believe me I'm not a prude, but the lack of self control.

Then (20.07.45) he notes that:

> Fratting is limited with girls fighting shy of talking too much to soldiers for fear of what neighbours might say and those that do frat are wearing tin knickers, so that you can't get at it, so the lads say who are in the know. I'm very fortunate having a temperament that can make me wait till P.G. I see you again.

There were other things to shock him (13.07.45):

> now that we are in the industrial part of Germany our eyes are being opened to the food problem, it seems pretty bad, kids are flocking to our cookhouse pouncing on swill and grabing at any thing on our plates before it goes into the swill bin and these children are well cleaned and not the

slum type … in Sicily we fed the kids but they looked starved and clothed in rags, so to see children, nicely dressed, doing that it makes you think and this is <u>Summer</u> God help them when Winter comes.

Sylvia was clearly concerned at the tone of her husband's letters, his apparent 'admiration for things German', so David (17.05.45) defends himself:

I had a good word to say for all the lands I've been in, each have its points of beauty, but Germany does strike one as being more English than any-where else … I've been to. I've taken the opportunity of doing a lot of walking, especially in the poorer districts, and now that the Fratt ban been lifted, I've been in their houses and had conversations with the people, there I'm afraid there is nothing to admire, unless you admire such things as slums, bad sanitation and anything ugly, so Nazi Germany made no effort at all to ellinate poverty, it built good roads instead.

His other preoccupations (13.07.45) were various: his demob date, 'the food problem' back home, checking whether Sylvia had seen Esther yet, giving Sylvia his head size for a jumper she was knitting and, the biggest item, his delight in a photo of Ruth that he had received:

Did I like it, I loved it, it was grand … I've put it on my bedside cabinet and there she is smiling at me and her little note as ever reminder that thank God I have a child who calls me Daddy.

He was still seeking (20.07.45) a small camera for Ruth's use only, 'it'll give her air of independence', and for himself he was 'on the list' for 'a real good camera, worth at least £10.0.0 for about 400 cigs', so he was glad that some 'fags', along with a parcel, were on their way to him.[6]

During this period Sylvia's mood clearly fluctuated. David expresses concern (14.07.45) about her 'depressed feeling' and was frustrated 'that I, at present can do nothing to help you'. He was also puzzled: 'don't you think dearest that the time for blues has gone?', since he would be home on leave and then back for good:

Still we are only human and there are times, tho, how much we steal ourselves, that it hurts where it pinches most. When you get like that, why don't you go places, not the same Whipps X [a local beauty spot] but go up West with Ruth, a walk in the Park tea at the corner house should break those blues up, they after all only temporary.

He tries to encourage Sylvia's mothering skills, such 'a darn good idea this telling stories and then making the children acting the parts'. Then tells of the promise of something he had come across and was sending home – it is 'new, hope they come in handy' – but he kept what 'it' was a secret.

By 17 July 1945 he was relieved to learn that Sylvia's mood had lifted and was moved by a comment from her about Mrs Rowe, the downstairs neighbour at Butterfields and an older woman, and says in his turn:

I've much to do and want a lot of time to do it in, when perhaps we both are the 'Rowes' ages we shall then look calmly at the face of death, knowing that we at least have lived, and that makes all the difference.

The swirl of thoughts and feelings at this point of his life is illustrated by his letter of 21 July. It is long and has a particularly warm start – 'My darling dearest Sylvia' – and there is an appreciation of the amount of mail he gets from her: 'I'm having to write nearly every day to keep up with you, not that I mind, Bless you a big <u>Bless</u>.'

He found it 'strange how I have a hankering after another child' but did not want it too soon, not 'till please God I'm finally shot of the army', but neither did he want to wait until he had settled on his future business, 'other-wise we'll be too old for that sort of thing'. Anticipating leave, he was thinking of putting in an application on 'religious grounds', presumably making a case for being with his family for the Jewish holidays of New Year and the Day of Atonement. He appreciated that this could mean that Ruth was in school for part of his leave, but then 'she did rather cramp our style'.

Despite this he sends Ruth a special letter (24.07.45), in careful capitals, to help cheer her up when he hears of her falling ill:

MY DARLING RUTH,

SO SORRY YOU HAVE CAUGHT THE 'RABBIT DROPS' OR MUMMY CALLS IT THE CHICKEN POX. HOPE YOU ARE FEELING A LOT BETTER.

IT'S A SHAME YOU HAVE TO MISS SCHOOL, AND YOU PLAY SUCH NICE GAMES THERE. SOON YOU WILL BE WELL AND BE ABLE TO GO BACK.

HOW IS THE GARDEN GROWING. WHEN I COME HOME PLEASE GOD I HOPE TO SEE PLENTY NICE FLOWERS.

WELL RUTHY PLEASE GET WELL QUICKLY FOR I'LL SOON BE HOME.

GOD BLESS YOU

I LOVE YOU VERY MUCH

DADDY
X FOR YOU
X FOR MUMMY
X FOR VICKY

The letter was sent with a sketch of 'RUTHY WITH THE SPOTS'.

David was also concerned (21.07.45) about the stories of long queues back in Britain and he returns to the issue of 'fratting', which was:

> not so bad. Young children go crazy about me, old women simply adore me, the girls and young women well – I'll leave it to your imagination

Not too much imagination, it seems, for he then asks Sylvia not to 'get so vexed about it, dearest mine'. He adds that his German is 'comming on a treat'; he could not only 'converse with a great deal of ease, I can even include jocular remarks', but:

I'd give a million to be just right be side you … this life is a dead loss … restrictions, the clothes you wear all tend to make it a punishment, not a pleasure … so what did I do, go to low dives, drink beer and spirit, pictures and more drinks, missed nearly all the real pleasures of sight seeing by being to busy to forget the life you were leading and danger attached.

In this continuing conversation about their attitudes towards the Germans, David becomes (24.07.45) quite formal:

Now for a little lecture. I don't like this they deserve it talk, if we come down to rock bottom, we too can claim some measure of guilt for this war, firstly for being apathetic in the pre war years on things that matter, secondly for using our vote with the least or no intelligence at all, the fault is the whole worlds, the democracies being stupefied and dictatorships being duped, hence war 1939, now is the time to rectify matters and not on the basis of they deserve it talk.

• *A Labour Victory: 'It Took my Breath Away'* •

The big news was the General Election (26.07.45). After spending the day with 'ears glued to the radio', David got the news that 'took my breath away': Labour had won a clear majority:

what a tribute to the intelligence of the people … if 1940 was their finest hour, then 1945 was their finest achievement. The results of the election was very well received by all of us, we are looking forward now to a planned society doing its best to abolish want and poverty, the road will be a hard one, but the courage that saw us thro the bitterest war of all times will be the same in the fight for freedom and plenty … Labour won because it offered a plan, for the little man, who had all to lose and nothing to gain if he reverted back to the old system … It also proved that democracy is not Churchill and that the will to win the war was the work of all and not one. a darn fine show.

He was further delighted by the news (31.07.45) of Bevin becoming Foreign Secretary, which 'should shake the old school tie diplomats' and then (04.08.45):

> not only ... Bevin but with the whole range ... as for Cripps he has a job that suits his legal mind. About time some thing other than 'God save the King' was sung any-where.

The fact that not all was well on the Labour front, however, is illustrated by his letters getting delayed, all down to the 'one day strikes of those crazy railwaymen'.

In contrast to this excitement, things back in Germany seemed very slow and routine; there was 'not a lot to write these days, things are slow, routine very drab, entertainment absolutely nil'. David busied himself (02.09.45) with ways of getting by, determinedly not 'fiddling', which he was very critical of, but he then gave an example of 'how things are done over here':

> I sold 10 cigs for 25 marks, gave it to a pal who was going on leave, to buy duty free cigs, 25 marks is worth 12/6 so he ordered 500 woodbines ... today I received those cigs, mind you its not every-body who will do this, but he is a special friend of mine. For those 500 cigs I can get £25-0-0 in German money, the difficulty is changing that money into English.

He also describes (12.08.45) a night out 'after duties'. He had 'a lie down on his "uncle Ned"' or 'bed', and woke and shaved to be off by seven o'clock 'to see what's doing'. The highlight of the evening could include 'dancing in a public house, drinking beer and listening to German dance bands'. If he danced with any young ladies he would then walk them home, but the good night was 'in the usual conversational style ... shaking hands'. None of this compared with the promise of being home:

> in another month at this time Sunday 2.30 pm I will be able to hold you in my arms, give you a nice big kiss and thank you very much for such a nice dinner, settle in the arm chair, switch on the radio and settle down to finish my 'Reynolds' that's if Ruth stops climbing all over me ... roll on my demob.

'Fratting' was also frustrating:

the kids pester you for chocolate and cigs for 'papa', the girls if you stop them, will only make a date with you on the understanding you bring them soap, chocolate and cigs or any spare food you can find, its all so embarassing this cadging. What I do is go for a mile or so out to a small mining village and chat to the old boys, who's only pleasure is to talk and smoke a good English cigarette, and in return I improve my German. I'm thinking that the aftermath of war is some times more tragic than the war itself. I've also been thinking about hosts of things, right thro my actual war experiences, I've seen plenty of German dead, now in the towns I'm seeing the living they have left behind. Scores of women who will never see their men again, children who will never know their fathers, the same position applies in England too, seen also about the streets are men without either arms or legs, Ruth's cryptic remark, that we are like the Germans also, rings very true … war curses all, is not respecter even if your case is a righteous one. I'm hoping a lot from the Potsdam big three meeting, they must arrive at a formula that will out-law war.

He ends:

oh yes … I'm glad that you told that certain Gentleman of 25 years or so, to paddle his canoe else-where. I'm having nobody muzzling in on my most precious territory. You should have told him that he might take my place out here, he'll find plenty of single frauliens that would please him no end for just a bar of chocolate. I like these blokes he couldn't find any single girl, and we have a surplus of about 2 million women, I wish I was there I'd have given him a good kick where the problem of women wouldn't concern him any more. Well after that you must think I'm jealous, I think I am, not too much so, for our love I think goes deeper then just possession, its understanding and that's what counts.

Perhaps this little scare encouraged David to pay attention to his domestic affairs, especially (2.08.45) with Sylvia approaching her thirty-first birthday; David hoped that this would be the last they would ever have to spend apart and looked forward to being with her for her eighty-first:

don't shudder at the age … for then we shall have the same love and respect as we have always had and even if we have no future the glorious past will have been <u>all ours</u>.

He enjoyed news of her and Ruth going blackberrying and visiting the zoo, and that Ruth could spell her name. Of Sylvia's talk of bungalows: 'they don't sound bad, but I prefer our own little flat, till something better comes along.' The 'something better' was not just their housing; talk of Ruth's maths skills prompts his joke that:

> we know one thing that confounds all books on arithmetic, that if one and one put together in a nice comfy position make three.

He busied himself (04.08.45) with bartering for an Afga camera, 'in good condition' and with 'a hell of a lot of gadgets attached', all for just '200 cigs', and he also sent some photos of himself, including one where he was on guard, 'I never knew I looked that smart', and a group photo with his fellow soldiers: 'they are a nice lot of fellows, I get on very well with them.'

• *The War is Over: 'What we Owe to them that Died'* •

The most momentous news was the end of the war, not just in Europe, but in Japan:

August 10th 1945.

My dearest Sylvia,

Well at long last this dam war is completely over the news did not come as a surprise, this new atomic bomb also the Russian declaration of war, made a war that might have lasted months, last just as many days.

What a relief it must be for this war weary and hungry world, what a relief for women, and wives and mothers who know now that they need no more to worry. What a wonderful chance for the world to start afresh, out of ruins to build and plan new cities, to gladen hearts with real things and make new world out of the decisions arrived at, thro the talks at Yalta, Sanfrancisco and then Potsdam, we must work now as hard as ever to reap out of the fields of dead a glorious harvest for the living, this is what we owe to them that died, let their small tiny crosses bear testimony to peoples, that the freedom they died for, lives for ever.

Well, loved one, bad flying conditions has put me in the position of not having heard from you for three days, and that dearest mine is very bad for my constitution, hoping to-morrow brings me a nice long letter.

How is my little Ruth, she should be out of her period of isolation [after her chicken pox].

News re demob look good, there is I think going to be a terrific speed up, I'm almost sure, you'll start the new year with a new life and with me Please God. I'll like that.

I've another good deal, have just given 300 cigs for a nice wrist watch for my-self, 10 jewels, it's a beauty, so for 500 cigs I'll have a tip top camera as well as a good watch and camera for Ruth and a small wrist watch for her too. I should be able to get them.

Well dearest mine it's very late, the actual time being 11 15 pm, so good night my darling mine, and roll on September, when we shall anew the love that we've had for a long time as I can pleasantly remember and let me end up with, it's been so nice knowing you intimately.

Well my bestest love to you and Ruth.

Yours always,
      David
X for you,
X for Ruth
X for Vicky

Sylvia raises a question in a letter that marks VJ Day (15.08.45), which provokes some thoughts about the atomic bomb:

> I'm not scared of the Atomic force, it'll be harnessed for the good of humanity, it will cause a silent revolution in mans mind that will astonish the world, you see ... I'm full of confidence in the future of the world and <u>ours</u>.

David was given the opportunity to celebrate the end of the war with some leave in Brussels and here (17.08.45) he was able to enjoy the weather, 'bright if cloudy', show off his ribbons and take photos, but also to renew his acquaintanceship with the city. He (18.08.45) went to '"shool" ... a beautiful temple and a very nice service, the organ played and a lovely quire'. Some of the soldiers were called up to the Torah. Here he met and talked with some Palestinian soldiers, some of the 5,000 stationed in the area, wearing the Shield of David. They were, David says, 'very nice fellows'.

The end of the war, and therefore David's war service, raised questions about his and the family's future. He had been thinking about changing the family name but (12.08.45):

> if Epstein and Einstein can still keep their names and still be famous, then I who hope to be great, can keep mine, the change of name represents an inferior complex and that kind of thing puts a mark on you right thro life. Imagine me a candidate for Parliament being asked by an 'anti-semite' why I changed my name, could I answer him truthfully, or would the truth shame me?

Turning to his work prospects, he thought Sylvia's suggestion that he continue with what he had been doing in the camp, tailoring, was 'a darn good idea'. Anticipating his accompanying her to synagogue, he looked forward to wearing khaki 'for your benefit', plus the metal ribbons which would show 'a grand splash of colour'. He adds that:

> I'm sure you'll want every-body to see what a hero your husband was and is, and as for my self, I'm equally as proud as you on my achievements. On

looking back, I've certainly helped in a big way to win this war, I certainly travelled some.

David notes Sylvia's concerns 'that its going to take a little time to get used to seeing each other day in and day out', but he asserts, 'honestly I don't think so'.

He goes on (28.08.45) to confront his future, looking forward to his next leave when he plans to have with Sylvia 'a serious talk … about the business of settling down to a job of work and how to make a living'. He had read Sylvia's warnings about the difficulties of resuming his shop, given coupons and the shortages of raw materials, but 'that doesn't worry me, I feel confidant that I can make a start and pull thru, it may be a struggle'. He plans to use his leave, ninety-six days of full pay, to do a refresher course on cutting and tailoring which would allow him to find work and 'wait for better times to commence my business'. Anticipating leave, 'I'm beginning to get worked up, not being able to sleep at night', and he worried at the news of Sylvia's 'silly little troubles', a term he immediately goes on to qualify: 'not silly, it does make you a woman … It will be nice having you completely well for the whole of the 12 nights [of his leave]'.

Before this, however, there was a problem to resolve. He had told Sylvia (21.08.45) about winning £5 from a bet on the Labour victory and had enclosed £1 of this for Sylvia to buy a bottle of wine. This was in readiness for toasting a present he had got for her, which was so beautiful that 'when you see it tears might spring to your eyes'. However, Sylvia had already heard of the win and David was left with some serious explaining to do. He (30.08.45) admonishes Sylvia for her 'horribly suspicious mind' on the 'trivial subject of one English pound note'. The delay in sending the money home was because it had to go by registered post which took 'three days', and he used a further underlining to urge Sylvia to 'please compare dates'. He comments on how hard this had been, for 'even tho I've a thick skin [I] also get hurt'. He returns to this at the end of the letter: 'sorry I told you off', but re-emphasises that she had misunderstood and got hurt unnecessarily 'and I love you too much to ever hurt – ever –'

The big news was that he should be home on leave by 5 September followed by his demob by the second week in December. On 1 September 1945 he rehearsed the journey home, leaving Friday morning from

Münster, arriving at Calais the next morning, embarking on the boat to England some time after dinner, thus arriving at Victoria by 6 p.m. and home at 6.45 p.m:

> I feel like two men and my feet don't touch the ground. I'm very much afraid that I'll be causing some damage when I see you both, I'll want to hug you till it hurts and bite lumps out of Ruth … Don't forget that bottle of wine, if it is possible, I've such a surprise for you.

• *Returned From Leave: 'Stark Raving Mad' as he Waits for Demob* •

David's next letters follow this period of leave. He still had an eye on how the Germans were faring and, with winter approaching, he lists (29.09.45) the rations for the civilian population:

> Bread, 4lb per week per person,
> Potatos, 4   ″   ″   ″   ″
> Butter and Fat combined is 75 grams per week per person,
> Meat, the same as butter and fat,
> Vegetables, not rationed but difficult to get,
> Coffee and tea unobtainable
> No tin stuff, no pickles … coal rather dubious wether civilians will get any.
> The Black Market is not a real proposition for supplies of food is so scarce
> … only the very rich can buy, all to-gether not a pretty picture.

He argues that:

> its recognised that the present ration allowances in Germany can only lead to semi starvation and malnutrition … even if we dub the entire German people as war criminals … [we should not] make them starve.

He praises the work of the Quaker relief organisations, 'but they can only touch just the fringe', and sees the answer in America and South America, countries that:

seem to have the surplus food supplies while England's position is such that we can only make suggestions.

He expresses his concern, (05.10.45) at press reports of how the Germans in the Polish part of Germany were being treated:

> it's making me so tired, we are slipping back very fast to pre war tragedies and mistakes. The failure of the big five is proving once again mistrust and power politics. Russia is very suspicious of America and wants buffer states and out-lets and you cant blame her, every-where there is talk of another war in twenty years time against Russia. Russia must be regarded as a great power and to be given power according to her status. England just can't see that in the Balkans, Russian politics must predominate, its part of Russia's economic plan and rightly so, hence the suspicion when England doesn't recognise the governments of Bulgaria, Hungary and Roumania. America is too prone to have every thing in the Pacific and is rather surprised that other countries should question it … Well, I suppose it'll work out OK in the end, its good to know that difficulties do face us and we just have to face up to them.

He was also prepared (15.11.45) to disagree with 'Monty', who wanted a big army in Germany because he anticipated trouble there in the winter:

> The people will suffer and hunger (if they must) with out a murmur, they are too 'bomb happy' and 'punch drunk' to do other-wise. I've spoken to many Germans on this subject, all say that they will manage to survive some how, all certain that after this winter things will be better, they'll pull thru, the bombing was worst, my conclusions are that Germany will be more peaceful than any of the allied countries.

He, meanwhile, was part of the Army of Occupation and he describes (20.11.45):

> a house searching party … they come every so often, not a pleasant job, we look mainly for fire arms, I suppose it must be done, we pick a home at random and search it, it generally scares the people, we get them out of

bed, [they] put on some kind of coat on over their night clothes and just get worried. We try to do it as nicely as it is possible, I'm usually glad when it's over, nothing has ever been found.

Nevertheless his main preoccupation was with his demob; he went (25.08.45) 'stark raving mad' when he heard this had been delayed, possibly until April:

If an atomic bomb droped among us, it wouldn't have caused as much damage … we fought a war and we are still sat upon, well its up to you wives to do something for us … shout for us to get out of the army.

He planned to contact his MP and had been sending off 'stinking letters … if I hurt them well its just too bad'. He adds:

if the Labour Party is going to nationalise industries with the same speed as demob, well the capitalists can sleep well on the their ill-gotten gains for the next four generations.

He was calmed (14.10.45) by Sylvia's chart to mark how long before he returned home and he responds to some warning words should he have strayed sexually:

Your a terror, so you would not be strong enough to forgive a very human frailty … well sweetheart mine don't let it bother you, I've kept off that path that leads to sex, I've found nothing that can take your place, either in my heart or in my mind but when I do, and I hope never, I'll take good care you'll know nothing about it, so it's up to you to keep young and beautiful … Seriously thou, I think I understand your point of view, as long as you remain steadfast in your love for me, I'll be the same with all the love that is with in me.

Regarding his potential name change, he had changed his mind and had gone so far as to request formally to take the name 'Winston'. He says that the forms are 'lying on the desk at the dept some place in the War office, all we have to do is wait'. He says that all 'the chaps' knew of his decision and were already calling him 'WINSTON' or 'CHURCH' for short. He later (16.10.45) reports that the CO had granted the application, after a delay caused by confusion about whether he completed the appropriate documents:

> My name never really worried me, being Jewish I was expected to have a foreign sounding name, to change it meant that perhaps I'd have some thing to hide, but on the other hand the name Weinstein has no real roots in our family. Dad's name was completely different until he came to England, why should we be saddled with a name the custom people gave Dad because they found it convenient.

He argues that, since the family had no Germanic connections, his actual origins are Russian, Polish or Slav. 'No it's about time it was changed.' He acknowledges that, having just learnt to spell and write one name, Ruth was 'indignant' about starting over again.

This talk of names and identities reminds David that he 'is concerned with a lot of things these days'. He wanted to forget about nationalities such as German, Serb, Slav, Latin, English: 'dead bodies looked alike, what-ever place they belonged to'. Having declared his opposition to nationalities, however, he then reacts to the news about Palestine:

> I've (tho not a Zionist) a sneaking admiration for what the Jews have done out there, they created a land where none existed before and every man is entitled to the results of his labour, the Arabs, meaning those wealthy Arabs, see a wealthy country going out of their hands, are creating a religious war, the Jews well are just being inpatient, and who can blame them.

These comments are given (19.10.45) a more personal edge after hearing from his friend Phil, who was himself Jewish, and was stationed in the Middle East where he had been involved in clashes between Jews and British troops. Phil, as a result, was 'rather perturbed over the Palestine trouble … He must feel rotten about the whole thing'.[7]

Alongside these considerations, Christmas was coming, with special regimental cards and the temptations of a gift shop. David had already put in an order, costing him £6-10-0, and 'I've bought nothing much'.

Nevertheless, he sent off twenty-four bars of chocolate, and, with more on the way, he advises, 'don't make pigs of your-selves'.

David describes (21.10.45) a Saturday night dance held by the regiment open only to girls aged between 18 and 55, with entry tickets costing 2 marks. He thought 'a good time was had by all', although he admits to getting 'easily bored' by dancing and preferred to sit and watch 'the antics' of others. It could become a weekly event providing rations were sufficient, 'other wise it'll be a case of holding dances while Germany starves, what a game'.

Following the news from Parliament, David (25.10.45) allowed himself a smile at Churchill's contribution to the demob debate, where he presented himself, now in opposition, as the soldiers' friend. He was delighted with the budget, praised even by the *Express* and *Mail*, so 'you'll see the Labour Party will run capitalism better than the capitalists'. He wanted Sylvia to tell their daughter 'that Daddy will see that where he can no poor little children will go hungry. Bless her heart.'

His enthusiasm was stoked by the 'tremendous gains' for Labour in the local elections (04.11.45), which meant that Nye Bevan could start his housing policy with the 'full co-opperatin from local councils'. Indeed, he regretted (06.11.45) that Sylvia had not voted communist:

a bright little spark like him on the council would have done the world of good, you could have omitted any Labour man, they probably all were the usual type of T.U. yes men.

As part of this reflection on the changing political mood he answered Sylvia's question (04.11.45) about whether 'the world [is] a better place because I've lived in it' with an unequivocal 'YES in big large capital letters'.

His demob came up again (25.10.45). His brother Alf looked to be out at near enough the same time as himself, which suggested 'a call for a nice dinner and dance some-where nice' and (04.11.45) he anticipated them both getting 'gloriously drunk' at a 'bumper Sedar night'. His good cheer with his family changed, however, (13.11.45) when some were actually discharged before him: 'All I can say is that there ain't no Justice.'

All this made his army life more frustrating. He could no longer get (09.11.45) the *Reynold's News* and found an alternative in *The People*, but this he found 'such a smug paper with a narrow outlook'. There was pride (25.10.45) when he told Sylvia to go to her copy of the regimental record book and to trace his activities with the 59th Regiment, which, for him, brought back memories, 'pleasant and other-wise'. Then, just two days later (27.10.45), and confined to billets by a gale, the reality of the present got to him:

> Nothing exciting to report these days, when you get food, clothing and shelter and nothing much to do the whole business of living passes you by, you just exist, that why I don't like the army, its too organised, it becomes dull, living becomes actually a thing of just existing and sleeping, there's no love, it has no place any where, it's not covered by army rules and regulations it's a thing apart, you pick it up where you find it, has no emotions except baseness, satisfies no spiritual appetites only physical, no wonder the army leaves in its wake rape and venereal disease, its whole principles make it so, it's a success only where men dont think, a rather damning inditment ... Ah well soon I'll be over with it and once more take my place in the ranks of those who want to make a better world, to live with the sound of laughter, real laughter and children playing, that's what I'm comming home to, can you not wonder why it can't come to soon,

Sylvia's comment about tears takes him to a different place too (09.11.45):

> You are right ... I think soldiers are continually wiping a tear away, silently but with feelings for the lads goes remembering a comradeship that was built on humour and friendship on a battle-field, for the lads who they left behind to carry on the rotten task of being a soldier. Life plays some scurvy tricks on people but I think I've gained wisdom, and broadened my outlook. I'm not any more the Dave that saw a world thru rosy spectacles, I'm not so soft, more enclined now to tell people what to do, then they tell me. I think it's all to the good.

Later (20.11.45) Armistice Day revived painful memories of:

> two chaps I shall never forget ... Frank Kitchen and Vic Blake, one I buried in the sands at Mareth, the other lies in a sodden field at Nijnegan, then

they are two of many, but they were very near to me and believe me to this day I feel their loss.

• *The German Jewish Family* •

David was learning more about the German experience from his contacts, including (04.10.45) his 'German employee', aged 46 and going 'by the good old German name of Ludwig Muller'. David found him to be 'a very nice chap' and 'a darn good tailor' and he was hoping for a reunion with his Jewish wife who he knew to be alive somewhere in the Russian occupied zone.

He also met (01.11.45) a Jewish family, consisting of 'a certain Herr Masson', his wife, a son of 18 and a girl of 20, and they invited him to their home, where he met other Jewish families. He found it strange that of the fifteen Jewish families in the town all had mixed marriages, the mother Jewish, the father gentile, but with the children brought up as Jewish. He learnt how common this was in Germany, and that it was condoned given the shortage of Jewish men, on the condition that the children were brought up as Jews. The girls all wore lockets inscribed in Hebrew and the 'Mogan Dovid', and 'as far as could be attempted, every thing was Kosher'. The men had all been sent to Austria as slave workers but, once released by the Americans, the Jewish Red Cross reunited the families:

> All had suffered privations, the children looked well but parrents had altered beyond recognition of photos they showed me of say 1936.

David sent off letters on their behalf to relatives in Cape Town, England and America.

Despite it being (10.11.45) 'a bit out of my way, rather a long walk and the weather has been rather bad', he visited again, taking a prayer book with him:

> they were delighted, it must be at least six years since they last saw one. The boy had forgotten most of it, the girl remembered a bit, they remembered quite a bit when I gave them the tune of 'Adown Alom' and others that

in the dim recesses of my mind came out on this occasion, it very much amused me afterwards that I sang at all, knowing my voice, but at the time I felt sad, soon I hope Jewish life will begin anew, free from intolerance.

He describes how on their return to the town they got the best accommodation, actually the home of a noted Nazi family, and a 'priority ticket and so not queue for any-thing they just walk up and get served'. As more and more of the Jews 'trickle back' (20.11.45) he had the chance to meet others and he anticipated some sad stories: 'perhaps the ending will be a happy one but it seems there are more black pages to be written'.

One German gentile, who did not know that David was a Jew, told him about a Jewish family returning to the town that had been their home for many years before the Hitler purges:

> Well they returned and were welcomed by the people of Verne with flow-ers, I'm not going to explain this, I'm just recording it as a fact. This world is full of strange happenings and glows and sparks of humanitarian instances.

• *Nearer and Nearer to Demob* •

There was a never-ending wait for demob and finding things to do to fill in this time. He turned down (23.11.45) the offer of a tailoring course; it was with a German firm so would have meant him spending Christmas away from the lads and giving up the job he was already doing, where:

> I'm in charge of all Jerry employees at R.H.Q see to the smooth running of the Tailoring dept., and see to the issuing of clothing and, what is more important, NO GUARDS, that means a night's sleep every night and I've a good billet.

For his time back home he had decided against going to 'a Pollytechnic (I hope that's spelt right)', preferring instead to look around for work, taking a few weeks 'to get into my stride'. Sylvia had been doing some sums (24.11.45) and if he was home by March he wondered what that meant for Terry's (the name for the anticipated new baby son) expected birth date. Catching up with family included some irritations, again with Sam who had some German money that was 'not worth the paper its printed on'. Sam had tried to get David to exchange it 'at a very reduced rate and I wasn't having any, it's useless'. Then there was the news (25.11.45) that the men who were at El Alamein, then Normandy, through to VE Day would get the commander-in-chief's certificate, 'that is from "Monty" himself'. David disarmingly acknowledges that this is the 'lowest form of award' but was pleased enough; it stands as a good record of his war:

> and the War Office thought it should have a special mention ... I'm the only one in R.H.Q. out of 140 men who is entitled to it.

Then came the news (27.11.45), a 'short scrawl' written in pencil: he was in 'a most excited mood' having swapped his leave with someone, so he was on his way home.

The break itself left him with the familiar mix of feelings. There were (16.12.45) the 'sudden gushes of emotion, the pent up feelings' which leave represents as opposed to being home fully – that time when there would be 'no <u>sweet sorrows</u> of parting, there will always be yesterday, today and tomorrow with you'. He was overall left (17.12.45) with 'some nice thoughts' remembered with 'a kind of half smile on my face' which he would live off for the next two months. Alongside were the regrets (20.12.45) of what he had missed, as represented by his daughter:

> its only by looking at Ruth and remembering that she was only 6 month old, that I shudder at the length of this terrible and shocking war.

He also wonders if fascism is defeated since he reads in the papers that Mosley has come back:

> it bewilders me, he and his click should be tried as war criminals ... while Natzis in Germany and elsewhere are being rooted out it doesn't seem logical that in England they are alowed the precious liberty that I and others fought and millions died for.

• Germany: Classes in Gardening, Plumbing and 'The Right Method for Banging in Nails' •

Meanwhile, back in the forces the authorities (20.12.45) were feeding their troops' minds as well as bodies, with classes in basic academic studies and also gardening, wireless repairs, painting and decoration, plumbing 'and the correct method to bang a nail in the wall'.

Christmas also offered comfort, with David describing (25.12.45) how:

> Xmas Eve started off with Dance and Cabaret Show, bags of beer till the early hours of the morning. I spent the first part of the evening with the Jewish family, then took the young girl on to the dance with us was another Jewish soldier, we stayed at the dance til 10.45 and then went back to the house had cake and coffee and left there for Home sweet home and bed at about 1 o'clock. this morning we were woke up by the Sgts with tea and rum, breakfast consisted of egg and bacon. Now we are doing nothing except read, talk, writ letters and wait for our Xmas dinner which will be tinned turkey, real geese, roast pork and potatoes, the usual Xmas pudding and custard, it should be a good doo To night again a dance and more beer, a strange thing is Xmas, all are trying to recapture a home and English atmosphere, behind this laughing and boozing exterior, there is a sadness, chaps all harking back in talk and thoughts, to wives, children mothers and sweethearts.

David took time to observe the German Christmas, how they made:

> quite a fuss over the Xmas Eve, all to church at 12 o'clock at night, children too, Christmas trees all evident in all homes, tho' there is precious little on them, like England it's a children festival completely.

Then (28.12.45) David received an unexpected present. Going to Ludwig for a 'pleasant tea and a chat', he was given 'an improvised illuminated address or ... epitath to be written on my tombstone in P.G. a hundred years time' (see full epitaph on p.185). David comments:

I was most touched and I think a little proud … I'm never happier than when I'm doing a little bit here and there of kindness, it kind of makes my little world go round and round.

Notes

1   As the fighting struggled to an end the question of the post-war settlement became increasingly urgent and anticipated the next stage of conflict. As one writer observed, 'everywhere in Europe the obsessions and polarities of the Cold War imposed themselves upon peoples' understanding and memory of the Second World War, but in few if any countries can they have done so with greater force or speed than in Greece' (Mazower, 2000, p.212). As it became clear that the Nazi troops would be forced to withdraw, Churchill was determined to support conservative elements in Greece and saw that this would be fiercely resisted by the communist-influenced resistance movement. 'The last German soldier left Greece on November 10, and clearly the British remained not to fight the Nazis but to settle Greek political problems', (Kolko, 1968, p.184) and armed conflict broke out between these troops and the resistance movement in December 1944.

2   David's mixed feelings towards the Germans he now encounters are not his alone. The mood is captured in the pocket-size booklet he carried: it had been issued in the name of Montgomery and entitled 'Letter by the Commander-in-Chief on Non-Fraternisation'. It warns 'You must keep clear of Germans – man, woman and child – unless you meet them in the course of duty. You must not walk with them or shake hands or visit their homes. You must not play games with them or share any social event with them. In short you must not fraternise with Germans at all.' In June, partly because of pressure from the Americans, this policy was modified and soldiers were then 'allowed to speak to, and play with, little children'. (see Meehan, 2001, for an extensive discussion of the British role in Germany from 1945 to 1950).

3   The authorities expressed rather more concern than David about this. Meehan (2001) describes how penicillin had to be flown in from Britain to manage the rising incidence of venereal disease among both the troops and German women who were resorting to prostitution, 'starving people could not afford morals' (p.114).

4   There was considerable concern at the numbers of former slave labourers, now DPs, Displaced Persons, who were either unable or unwilling to go home to Russia or Poland. Confronted by 'marauding gangs murdering, raping and pillaging, driven by hunger and by vengeance' (Meehan, 2001, p.39), Montgomery authorised offenders being caught in the act to be shot on sight.

5. Between March and July 1943 'Bomber' Harris had unleashed on Hamburg nearly 800 aircraft in 18,000 individual missions dropping a total of 58,000 tons of bombs. A four-night raid created a firestorm that 'burned to cinders the heart of the great North German port covering 62,000 acres' and killed 30,000 people (Keegan, 1997, pp.355–6). Meehan (2001) quotes the poet Stephen Spender: 'In the destroyed German towns one often feels haunted by the ghost of a tremendous noise' (p.31).

6   The black market was fuelled by such dealings and as such the cigarette represented 'probably one of the biggest single threats to financial stability in the country' (report of the Economic Branch, cited by Meehan (2001, p.116)) and created what a British MP termed an 'appalling moral vacuum' (Meehan, 2001, p.117).

7   This 'trouble' refers to the British mandate in Palestine, where the Jewish/Zionist settlers were demanding an increase in immigration into Palestine as part of their demand for a 'Jewish National Home', and where the Arabs were equally fiercely resisting such pressures, being concerned for the loss of their homes and territory. Both sides were fighting each other, and the British soldiers were in the middle. David's ambivalent feelings were shared by many of the 'left'. The Left Book Club text *The Jewish Question* by Sacks (1937), in a chapter headed 'The Promised Land', repeats the Zionist claim for a Jewish state, where Jews could feel safe and be respected, and says

that 'the argument is unanswerable'. Sacks then goes on to argue, however, that '*they have arrived at this solution too late*' (emphasis is original) (pp.73–4), now that Arab nationalism had become a major force, and no Jewish state could be secured 'under the threat of war and civil war' (p.81).

Six

1946

DISAPPOINTMENT, SHOCK AND
ANTICIPATION OF THE FUTURE

THIS PERIOD WAS ABOUT treading water. Sylvia writes that she has had a period, so is not pregnant, and gives news of crime and disenchantment of families when they are reunited. David frets about his delayed discharge, managing his frustration through educational classes and imagining being at home, gardening, going to shows, helping out at Ruth's birthday parties. The reality of life in Germany is brought home to him by finding the body of a civilian who has committed suicide and bidding farewell to the German Jewish family who had 'adopted' him. Then he gets his wish and on 2 March 1946 he pens 'positively my last letter from Germany' and prepares for his journey home.

David hoped that this would prove 'a momentous year for both of us' (29.12.45), although it was initially dispiriting. Sylvia reports two news stories, one of a robbery, and David responds, 'those kind of petty thieves want whipping', and another about women already bored with their husbands returned from the war. Concerning this, David asserts that 'we are a couple in a million ... ours was a love affair ... our little adjustments will come without any bother'. Sylvia had also had her period so he was sorry about Terry: 'still he is always there when we want him (I hope).'

He describes (02.01.46) his New Year's Eve, spent:

very quietly, had a few beers, went to the dance, bags of 'blokes' very drunk, went back to the billet and then spent New Year Eve with you all at home thru. the medium of the radio, stayed up till 1 o'clock, heard the chimes of Big Ben and went to bed very home sick, I did miss you such a lot. Woke next morning and gave myself a hearty kick, pinch and punch and wished myself a very Happy New Year and hell I feel a lot better.

Then (03.01.46) he writes of how the previous day he had had a 'most terrifying experience'; he had gone:

into the shoe repair shop to give the German workers some boots and there he was strung up with some wire he had hanged himself, it shook me a little, the first thing I did was to call for help and then I had the unpleasant task of cutting him down, he sure was dead, hung himself on New Years day. I certainly see life. He was a pleasant man of 55 years of age, he had a wife and children, he left one note to the C.O. appologising for commiting the act on his premises, other-wise it's a mystery, well I've seen plenty of bodies and now I've seen a suicide.

Such dramas apart, David's preoccupation was with home and becoming a family man again. Thus he wanted (06.01.46):

to get cracking … I want to see to that garden and Feb and March is the ideal time to start turning the earth over and a get a lawn going and the sides tidied up.

He enjoyed hearing that Sylvia was booking tickets for various shows like *The Glass Slipper* and *Jack and the Beanstalk*, for Ruth primarily, 'and it makes a break for you too'. Then (09.01.46) he was literally counting the minutes:

It's now 6.30 p.m. I'm now imagining that you are still talking over your cup of tea at Lyons abut the show you've all seen, Ruth full of chatter and excitement and you all saying it was a nice show and we had a nice time thanks to David, I hope I'm right.

He wonders (13.01.46) if 'we' should now book up to see *Perchance to Dream*; he liked the idea of Ruth 'seeing decent shows and good music … it's the intelligent thing to do'.

With (17.01.46) Ruth's birthday pending on 31 March, he was 'thanking God' that he would be home to celebrate it, ready 'to join in the fun and help you with the washing up and entertaining the little guests'. He was fine with Sylvia spending £30 on furniture for Ruth; this seemed 'quite reasonable … these days', and he looked forward to seeing it and recognising that it was 'another stage in her life'. Then he worries with Sylvia (23.01.46) about rationing:

> It's a darn shame, seeing that the weather is so cold and bodies must have some-thing solid inside them. I can't understand your meat ration, what does the butcher say? Just nothing, or shrugs his shoulder. Don't worry about me. I'll be O.K. two can starve as cheaply as one so we'll manage you'll see so please don't worry, things will get better.

There were more concerns over budgeting (24.01.46) to the extent that:

> Now I'm going to tell you off – why didn't you buy that corset and also book for 'Perchance to Dream'. I'm saving my money as fast as I draw it, and believe me you can afford at least to buy Ruth Wellingtons and also corset and book for seats.

Clearly there were some limitations to his involvement with home. Sylvia had been using David (01.02.46) as a parenting threat, in his words 'a bogey man', and he was amused at Ruth's burst of outrage. He warmed to 'her independent little soul [that] rebelled at the thought that I should in any way interfere with her'. He wanted to 'rather help' and acknowledged that 'I've got to gain her love and confidence, you already have it'. David reassured Sylvia regarding the problems of readjustment of father and child, and refers to four lectures he had attended given by 'a very good psychologist' on the subject of the 're-adjustment of a soldier to his wife, child and home life'.

He had (09.02.46) been busy preparing for home in other ways. He had sent Ruth a handbag, 'made by friends', and provided a sketch of a coat for her that was almost ready, 'real tailored' and 'heavy weight' and, given that it was 'on the big side', it would last next winter. Sylvia had asked for advice on selling a pram but he was happy to leave that decision up to her: 'its your pidgin.' Sylvia tells of a returning soldier who was having a hard time of it, which prompted David's concerns for himself:

> army life taught you nothing and made you forget what you did in Civvy Street, the system promotes bad training for independence and self reliance, you've got to start all over again.

He adds that he might be OK, 'they never did regiment me'.

A soldier's life was still a busy one. He had (20.01.46) been a referee for a football game between the NCOs and the gunners – 'I had a good time blowing whistles' – and (11.02.46) he was pleased that the regimental magazine published 'a littery effort of mine'. He enclosed a copy, explaining that:

> I let my imagination run riot but it was as near the real thing as could be written in a few words (I expect) a few pokes at my rather vivid and graphic style of writing. One bright 'spark' ... wants to know what a cloud of doom looks like ... every-body has told me it was the best effort up to date in the series I'll never forget.[1]

There were also (08.01.46) the education classes; each man was supplied with exercise books and the classes were held in a building a pleasant half an hour's walk away. For maths (08.01.46), the men divided into three groups, one for those that knew a little, another for those that knew nothing and a third for 'those that know nothing at all'. This last group was the class he joined where, along with twenty others, he did simple fractions. The English class had a 'sylabus [that] is quite edifying', although he was 'rather perturbed at the spelling Bees', and he was also learning German.[2] All in all:

> its making me use brains which for a long time has lain dormant, its all to the good ... its all so nice, education is a grand thing.

He especially enjoyed being called 'Mr' and not 'gunner', a simple act that made his thoughts more 'independent'.

David was surprised (17.01.46) by his success. He passed fractions and he was now 'well thru multiplication of decimals', clearly with some help from Sylvia since he was using her 'method, it is easy as you say'. Such was his confidence that he was not even worried about any future spelling bees, adding:

> Any-way I'm considered one of the bright boys. I excel in discussion groups on History and Political subjects, this morning I led the discussion on the U.N.O. and world power politics and after speaking for ½ hour got quite a big ovation, was personally thanked by the instructor for leading the discussion so well ... believe me most chaps are looking at me with a great deal of respect. I'm pleased. I like to do well.

He elaborates on this (23.01.46) with his story of how, in a discussion group on Trade Unions, the lecturer got into such a muddle when challenged that David:

> answered the question for him, I aparently made it so clear that a spontaneous clapping rewarded my effort, it quite embarassed me ... I then led the opposition to a motion: 'That this house is of the opinion that for insuing future world peace, Germany will for ever be divided up in small Zones'. I hope one day to enjoy putting into practice things that for so long I have preached.

There was also (04.02.46) frustration where, in one debate, he was clear that he had 'won the <u>argument</u>' but lost to the 'ignorance and muddled thinking' of his opponents. Nonetheless, he defends himself against the 'smug' comments from Lou, who suggested that:

> I didn't explain myself well in the language they understood [but] I've been living with these men or types like them for nearly 5½ years – if I can't speak their language now, I never will.

Rather than debating with trade unionists or political thinkers, 'the already converted', David was proud to be with:

> the cross section of England, toilers, like miners, road sweepers, engineers, office workers and the like ... blokes who's only interest lies in the back page of any newspaper or the spicy bits in the 'News of the World'.

David refers to the regimental paper, how it carries his letters and mentions his name. He even made the front page when he found the dead German cobbler: 'it shows that I'm particularly famous a personality in the Regt.'

He stayed busy with his wider contacts, so when he asks (17.01.46) for parcels, especially with 'coco and coffee', this was not for himself but rather to give away:

> these people, Jewish and half Jewish are making a tremendous fuss of me and I'd like to repay it in kind. One family is making Ruth a dress ... the Menzle family have already given something for the house.

This turned out (04.02.46) to be a set of antlers and the badge of the pre-Hitler police force which, when sent home in a parcel, had obviously rather startled Sylvia, but she eventually decided to put it over the sideboard. David assures her that 'it's the real "goods"', which he had admired while at the home of one of his Jewish friends and the next week they presented it to him as a gift. This was followed up (17.02.46) by Ruth's coat; David had got the material and Ludwig had made it up:

> and left a note in the pocket to little Ruth from her German uncle ... The biggest surprise is a <u>gold</u> ring with setting of two little pearls and a ruby in the centre. I'm quite taken with it, belonged to a Jewish woman and she wore it when she was a child so its very old and had sentimental value but she wanted Ruth to have it, as it was the only way she could show her thanks to me. When I go there'll be plenty of tears ... I'm just one of the family to the whole of the Jewish community of Bochum, or whats left of them.

• *Still Waiting for Discharge: Getting out is 'A Ticklish Job'* •

Waiting for the actual discharge proved difficult and the anticipation was keen. He had, he points out (20.02.46), been in the army since 20 November 1940:

so let me go with no regrets, duty done ... 1101886 will cease to exist in any shape or form and now dies easily and painlessly, it now belongs to History and to things forgotten. I'll dedicate it to the sands of the desert, the vinyards of Sicily, the fields and woods of France Belgium Holland and Germany, for that is its rightful place, it belongs to me no more, it'll be only remembered that it won for me a place to live with my wife and children in a free and unfettered world.

He was ready to leave Bochum (22.02.46), where snow must have fallen fast over the preceding twelve hours, leaving the town looking prettier than ever, and effectively hiding:

the war games of this town, covered the dirty streets, hid its rubble and bomb craters and innocently making it appear beautiful

He writes that the next day the sun would be out and bringing Bochum back to life again, 'with all its sores exposed'. He compares it to the virgin bride who wakes the next morning 'striped of her Bridal gown [when] she may feel like a scarlet woman'.

It was the weather that served (25.02.46) to delay his demob even further, leaving him in a 'nasty mood ... It didn't take em long to get me in, getting out is a ticklish job'. The army might have been good with anything that came under the King's Rules and Regulations, but 'it's human emotion that the army knows nothing about'.

The inevitable, however, could not be delayed forever. By 1 March 1946 he was all packed, his pay made up 'and one ticket and release book is nicely tucked away in my inside pocket'. He became 'quite civvy minded', anticipating the changes at home, looking in the paper at the entertainment charts and the 'positions vacant' column, although he adds, in brackets: 'I shudder at the thought of work.' However, before all this he had to face the 'really unpleasant task' of saying goodbye to his Jewish friends. They had planned a farewell party at the home of the Manzels and they were expecting about twenty people:

> Mrs Manzel has been like a Mother to me, she is baking a cake for my journey in case I shall be hungry, so much like my own Mother. I've promised to write them very often and P.G. one day you and I will visit Germany and see them, yes, I certainly have made friends all over the world, what an experience.

His next letter (02.03.46) was in something of a race for he was off the next day and was wondering if he or the letter would be the first home. He describes the journey to come; on Sunday he would:

> leave by truck 10.45 to Krefield, from Krefield by train on all night travell to Tornay Belgium, there we change our money and stay the rest of the day, again travell all night to Calia, getting there in the early hours of Tuesday morning, then some time Tuesday morning or in the early afternoon by boat to Dover and then on-to our Demob Centre which will London. I have hopes of spending Tuesday night with you. If not a certainty for Wed night Please God.

His even more than usual idiosyncratic writing is explained as 'a scribble and I cant concentrate, your probably feeling the same way'. And he ends on a note of celebration and triumph: 'positively my last letter from Germany.'

....

Notes

1 The cutting is from the 'Letters to the Editor' column of *The Medium*. It is signed Gnr. D. Weinstein and reads as follows:

> October 23rd 1942 brings back to me a flood of memories I shall never forget.

We gunners were feverishly active, digging dummy gun positions to throw sand in Rommel's eyes. By the evening of the 23rd we were ready.

The balloon was going up. A dead silence. The darkness was descending like a cloud of doom. We were all tensed, poised, No. 3 with hand on firing lever, No. 1 nervously fidgeted with his programme sheets.

At the shrill of whistles, still figures silhouetted in the desert gloom, sprung to life, the word 'FIRE' rung out like a bell through the gun detachments.

The flap had started, El Alamein was on. The Gods of War laughed their loudest. Gun flashes lit the night like a gorgeous firework display.

The roar of guns lifted the very earth, the rumbling of tanks increased the intensity of this war-like scene. It gripped you.

I didn't know then but I had helped to make history.

This provoked a flurry of good-humoured responses in the next edition (13.02.46). One respondent refers to the phrase 'balloon going up' and asks: 'Was this due to the hot air? A lot of this commodity seems to have preserved for subsequent use' Another notes the claim that '"tailor" Weinstein had been making history', adding: 'That is one job that can't be sent back for alteration.' Lastly, a reader suggests that the letter belonged on the sports pages since it is apparently reporting a game 'played with balloons and sand' and how 'unsporting [it is] to throw sand in anybody's eyes. No wonder the whistle blew.' The editor adds: 'What about it David? Are you going to take it lying down? Surely you can sew this little lot up.'

2 David's primer is entitled *German From Scratch: Bill und Jock in Deutschland*, issued by Modern Languages for the Services. There is no publication date but it was clearly popular since David's was the fourth edition.

Seven

AFTERTHOUGHTS

THE CORRESPONDENCE ENDS ABRUPTLY in this frantic, triumphant
'scribble' that announces David's discharge home. He was
in such a rush that there is no neat summary or concluding
thoughts from either David or Sylvia, so this final chapter seeks to provide
something of that and to look ahead, giving a sense of 'what happened
next' to the Weinstein family and the impact that stumbling across these
letters had on their children.

As a final comment on the letters themselves, there are many stories about
the Second World War: academic studies, political commentaries, personal
accounts, novels, plays and films, and more. Each and every one is valued
and valid, representing what has been called a 'big picture' of 'a nation
united in courageously facing a common enemy' and, within this, there
are also many 'short stories, the details of peoples' varied experiences
of war that complicate and nuance that picture' (Gardiner, 2004, p.x).
We believe these letters are a further set of 'short stories' with their
own unique mixture of complications and contradictions. Some of the
experiences related in the letters will, of course, be familiar to the modern
reader, but they were shocking and new to David and Sylvia, and in their
telling we are helped to see anew the privations and excitements of the
battlefield and of a ravaged Europe, and the struggle of daily life back in

Britain beneath the ever-present threat of bombs. There is also the Jewish dimension to their story. David's running commentary on all that he sees around him, especially his observations in Germany, are not just those of a British soldier in the Army of Occupation, but also of a Jew, as the horror of the Holocaust begins to emerge. Sylvia is perhaps less explicit about this dimension, but it is there in the daily descriptions of her life in her close-knit wider family and the practice of her religion and the meaning that they hold for her.

In terms of 'what happened next', David did return to Butterfields, the council flat in Walthamstow that Sylvia had been carefully making ready for the reconstituted family. The much-awaited son arrived in March 1947, and was named not Terry but Jeremy. David returned to work, in tailoring, and then, several years later, set up in business, a menswear shop, first with Sam, the brother-in-law who features so often in his letters, and then on his own. Both of these shops were in Leytonstone, in East London, and only a mile or so from the business that was bombed out back in 1941. Sylvia helped occasionally in the shop and worried over the accounts, but she saw her main role as maintaining a traditional Jewish home, lighting the Friday night Sabbath candles, cooking kosher meals and observing the festivals; all those elements that David had longingly anticipated in his letters. When the family moved from Butterfields to a new council estate, still in Walthamstow, David and Sylvia became active in that community, helping to start the Residents' Association, with Sylvia taking on the role of treasurer and David taking on various positions, and both of them were involved in producing a monthly magazine. They remained Labour Party activists, which sustained the concerns that are reflected in the letters about the wider political picture and what awaited the German population that David had seen struggling to survive, about Palestine, the civil war in Greece and the bombing of Hiroshima – all the events that would continue to haunt the world, 'shading into the peace', as Gardiner puts it (2004, p.x). More immediately, politics meant running the committee rooms at election times and while David never achieved his parliamentary ambitions, he did become a councillor and then fulfilled the promise he had made to make Sylvia 'a beautiful Mayoress' when he was chosen, in 1967, to be the first Jewish Mayor of Waltham Forest. He remained a councillor right up to his death. A fortune teller in Egypt may have promised David that he would live to be 83, but he actually died aged 64 of heart disease, helped along, perhaps, by the generous supply of 'cigs' that were a mainstay of his army life. Sylvia survived him by many years, dying aged 94 in 2009, the doctor's certificate giving the cause of death as 'old age'.

Interestingly, given the subject of this volume, the Second World War was never an especially significant discussion point or event in our family history. There were various indications of David – dad's – life as a soldier around the house. A photo of him in his uniform was prominently displayed in the main living room, as well as a little, battered toddler's shoe that was baby Ruth's which had been rescued from the wreckage when the family business and home had been bombed out; dad carried this with him throughout the war as a good luck charm. On the wall in the front room was a pair of antlers mounted on a wooden plaque that also had a badge of some German official. There was a large wooden ship with canvas sails puffed out and a flag flying. We knew dad had brought all of these back from the war, along with the copy of the German-language *Mein Kampf*. In a drawer there was a collection of memorabilia, including two large books of photographs and commentaries, one called *The Army at War Tunisia* and the other announcing itself as *The Official Record in Pictures and Map of The Battle of Europe*. There were also copies of *The Medium*, the weekly newspaper of the 59th (4th West Lancs) Medium Regt RA. There was also a Yellow Star with the word 'Jude' in Hebraic-style letters. Alongside dad's army medals was a little box decorated with a church and ringing bells, and inside the message 'TO PREVENT YOUR CARD FROM BECOMING SOILED, PLACE THIS MAT ON TOP OF THE CAKE'. All this was incongruous given its contents, which were two swastika badges, one black on a white background ringed with a bold red, the other also black on white but with a gold surround and set on a blue cross.

The war, although present in these ways, was never a discussion point as such. As a family we went to Whitehall to watch the annual CND Aldermaston march, but not to attend the November Armistice parade; dad liked to watch war films on the television but no more, it seemed, than westerns. Occasionally old army comrades, Phil or Paddy, would visit and perhaps the old soldiers would reminisce while the wives chatted and the children of both families played together, but neither of our parents talked about their experiences with us, the children; or perhaps it was simply that we never asked. We are not aware, either, that they talked about it between themselves and certainly dad, for all the promises in his letters, only once took mum back to the sites and sights of his wartime experiences: a holiday in Sicily.

So this is all by way of saying how surprised we, Ruth and Jeremy, were on discovering the world that opened up for us when we found the letters that were the bulk of the correspondence that dad and mum exchanged during the war years. Ruth was the first to find a box, packed full of frail envelopes and with mum then in her late eighties and growing increasingly frail, both physically and psychologically; Ruth would pick out the occasional letter as a sort of reminiscence exercise and mum would sigh and shrug as she read them, in the same way as she would when looking at old black-and-white photographs. It was not until 2006, when our mum's condition so deteriorated that she needed residential care and we started the painful business of clearing out the family home, that we came across another box and realised that we had something like 700 letters in total. Ruth took these home with her and started the process of reading and transcribing them; Jeremy took longer to come round to the task, and it was not until a year or so after our mum's death in 2008 that he started looking through the second box. However, from that date onwards, both of us became absorbed in the letters, discovering a whole world and a level of intimacy which was at times very moving, disturbing and always engaging. For Ruth it has been deeply affecting to have such vivid details of her early childhood and to read the love her parents had for her. For Jeremy it has also been fascinating to see how firm his parents held to the belief that they would have a son and that he represented a hope for the future. It has also shed light on a crucial period in their parents' life, all the more striking for how little it was then talked about in the post-war years.

Having started to transcribe the letters, we then wanted to develop and shape them so that they became a narrative and a dialogue. Initially this was for our own interest and to share with surviving family members, but we then began to imagine a wider readership and considered whether we could or should turn it into book form. We were encouraged in this by various family members and friends but also, we came to believe, by dad and mum themselves. Mum had, after all, kept those two little boxes safely over all the years while dad had written about how his letters could be 'the basis of one of the greatest books yet to be written' and that mum's letters, likewise, could be 'printed ... and title[d] "The Memoirs of a soldier's wife"' (02.02.43). Nonetheless we cannot be sure what dad and mum would have made of our efforts to make public what were their private letters. Perhaps, to revert to Yiddish, they would see it as a '*chutzpah*', or barefaced cheek, perhaps a '*mitsvah*', a good deed. Hopefully dad would have been, to use a favourite phrase, 'tickled pink', while mum might have given one of her self-deprecatory shrugs. We will never know and can only hope that they would have appreciated our attempts to understand and honour their lives.

• In Memory of my English Colleague •

'The noble and pure friendship also may mean absently very much; to feel that also remote one is thought of, enlarges and doubles their own existence'

Friedrich von Schiller

It seldom happens in life to meet men worthy of a dedication. In you my dear English colleague Weinstein, I found such an one.

You always had an ear for the matters we must endure in Germany.

Your attitude was collegial, moving me very deeply in my heart. Allied in our destiny we exchanged psychical suffering each other and quieted by the way, the war, went, we stroke the balance.

As I am unable to express my thank in other way, please take as a sign of my thank this dedication with you into your home with the certainity that you mean much for me and that you have good memory in me.

I wish you further on fortune and contentment in the circle of your family.

Your colleague

Ludwig Müller
Germany, Bochum
in December 1945

LIST OF ILLUSTRATIONS

BIBLIOGRAPHY

THE MAIN INTENTION OF this volume has been to allow the letters to speak for themselves; David and Sylvia's words should be enough. Since the reader may find it useful, at times, to see something of the broader context, throughout the text there are references to wider reading.

For the Jewish East End there is Jacobs' *Out of the Ghetto, My Youth in the East End, Communism and Fascism, 1913–1939* (Simon, 1978) and linked to this, but specifically for **Sylvia's family background**, Lou Ryder's 1994 unpublished memoir *I Remember Father*. The other books referred to were published by the Left Book Club, and included *The Jewish Question* by Sacks (1937) and *The Yellow Spot: The Extermination of the Jews in Germany*, which has no author but carries a foreword by the Bishop of Durham (Gollancz, 1936), which might now only be available in second-hand book shops. The reference to the BUF, and the continuing fight against the Mosleyites after the war, is *The 43 Group: The Untold Story of their Fight Against Fascism* by Morris Beckman (Centerprise Publications, 1992).

For life on 'the Home Front' a powerful collection of stories and experiences is provided by Juliet Gardiner's *Wartime Britain, 1939–1954* (Headline Book Publishing, 2004). A powerful insight into the lives of women is also provided by Virginia Nicholson in *Millions Like Us: Women's Lives in War and Peace 1939–1949* (Viking, 2011).

For a general history of the war there is J. Keegan's study, *The Second World War* (Random House, 1977), while R. Kee's *1945, The World We Fought For* (Hamish Hamilton, 1985) focuses on the final stages and the emerging political perspectives.

For the Eighth Army there is the undated Ministry of Information booklet *The Eighth Army* (HMSO); and for a history of the **war in North Africa**, John Bierman and Colin Smith's *Alamein, War Without Hate* (Viking, 2002). An insight into the experience of a gunner is offered in William Styron's *The Suicide Run* (Jonathan Cape, 2010).

For the Army of Occupation see Patricia Meehan's *A Strange Enemy People, Germans Under the British, 1945–50* (Peter Owen, 2001).

For the political dimension there is Gabriel Kolko's classic text *The Politics of War* (Vintage Books, 1968), and the more recent text *The Politics of Retribution in Europe. World War II and its Aftermath*, edited by I. Deák, J.T. Gross and T. Judt, and carrying the article cited above on 'The Cold War and the Appropriation of Memory: Greece after Liberation' by M. Mazower (Princeton University Press, 2000). Kee's text, cited above, focuses on the latter stages of the war and the political hopes in the UK that so engaged both Sylvia and David.

INDEX

If you enjoyed this book, you may also be interested in...

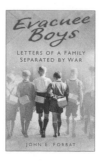

Evacuee Boys

JOHN E. FORBAT

Having been living in England since 1936, John and Andrew Forbat': Hungarian family became Enemy Aliens at the onset of the Secon: World War. Aged 11 and 14, the two brothers were evacuated to a disadvantaged part of Wiltshire, to find themselves in straitened circumstances far from home. Letters and diary extracts make *Evacuee Boys* as full a record of war-torn Britain as one family could provide.

978-0-7524-7123-5

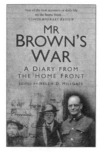

Mr Brown's War

EDITED BY HELEN D. MILLIGATE

In this book, as well as describing the development of the war, Brown captures a vivid image of life in wartime Britain, with rationing, blackout restrictions, interrupted sleep, the prospect of evacuation and the enormous burden placed on civilians coping with a full-time job as well as war work.

978-0-7524-5931-8

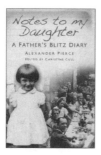

Notes to my Daughter

ALEXANDER PIERCE

When Christine Cuss (née Pierce) was born in 1934, her doting father began a journal addressed to her. At first he recorded everyday details such as first teeth and family holidays, but as the 1930s progressed his words took on a more sinister tone, as Europe and the world prepared for war. The sentiments expressed in these loving entries open a window into the extraordinary life of an ordinary family.

978-0-7524-5554-9

Even to the Edge of Doom

WILLIAM & ROSALIE SCHIFF & CRAIG HANLEY

By turns riveting, harrowing and moving, and featuring illustrations from the United States Holocaust Memorial Museum archive, *Even to the Edge of Doom* is powerfully narrated by Craig Hanley and tells the story of two young lovers who manage to stay alive, against all odds, and find one another again at the end of the war.

978-0-7524-6039-0

Visit our website and discover thousands of other History Press books.

www.thehistorypress.co.uk